Chapter 1: Chapter 1: Awakening

...

You are Shinji, an orphan with no last name and nothing to your name. Your seat was to the back of the classroom, and while you weren't dead last in here, you still were very much behind the likes of Sasuke Uchiha. You felt a little envy in your heart at the last Uchiha, he was ahead by a long shot to everyone in the class.

Unlike him, if someone were to ask the teachers what you are good at, they would say that Shinji was average in almost everything. It wasn't a bad thing, but neither was it good. You didn't want to be just average. Well, nobody wanted to be just average either, and if they could change it they would.

Suddenly, you hear the sound of the classroom door creaking. Iruka came into the class, he had a frown on his face, showing that his day hadn't started in a good step. You could guess why that was so.

He was a little later than usual and you could reckon why by the tied-up yellow-haired ball of energy in his arm.

He drops the wriggling student on the ground and turns towards him. "Naruto, how many times did I tell you?! Not only did you miss class but also went and vandalized the Hokage Statues!!"

Naruto smiled confidently, and you guessed that he would have given you a thumbs up if he could get out of the ropes. "I am going to become the greatest Hokage! Better than any that came before me!"

Wow... Yeah, you didn't believe that at all.

Unlike others, who seemed to hate him for no reason, you didn't hate Naruto and even found some of his pranks entertaining sometimes.

But, at the same time, you were looking at this from a logical standpoint, Naruto simply didn't work hard enough to be Hokage. His Taijutsu was almost nonexistent, even though he had pretty good stamina. His Ninjutsu... he couldn't even do the simple Clone Jutsu, and to top it all off, his grades were horrendous. You didn't even know one academic subject where he passed.

Naruto was a guy who liked pulling pranks more than training. That was your conclusion for now, and it was too late to change that now. Hard work is about consistency, not just one moment in time like a day or a week.

"Naruto!" Iruka yelled out the young blonde's name again and punched him on the back of his head. Stopping Naruto's grandeur speech. "Tomorrow is your graduation exam. So you can't be doing things like this anymore."

You almost sighed at the situation. Initially, it had been entertaining, but now almost every other day Iruka would bring Naruto to class and reprimand him for something or other. There was a reason why the children didn't like Naruto, well, one was his annoying pranks and the other was how adults told their kids to stay away from him.

While you were curious about what secret Naruto had, a chill crawled down your spine just thinking about trying to find out a secret like this. A Ninja village wasn't something you could waltz around like that and try to investigate.

With a sigh, you get rid of such thoughts for now. Some secrets were better not known.

After clearing your mind, and ignoring Iruka's yells, you couldn't help but think about tomorrow and feel a little nervous.

Though you could use the three basic Jutsu like almost everyone in the Class could. From what the older years usually said, as long as you could perform the three basic Jutsu, then you would pass. The academic grades didn't matter as long as you weren't completely failing like... Naruto, and maybe Kiba. The latter at least was in most of the classes, in body, because his mind was in dreamland most of the time, as he usually slept like a log through most classes.

But you were sure that in the end, Kiba would graduate. Clan kids would always graduate since even if they somehow failed, their family members would be enough to pick up the slack and make a ninja out of them.

Orphans like you on the other hand, and normal civilians, were a different deal. You didn't know the exact premise, but no one that you knew from the orphanage ever became a ninja in the last two years. Sure, there were many orphanages throughout Konoha due to the Nine-Tails attack, so some of them probably became true Genin.

But still, you were confident that there must be something more to the Genin Test than just using the three normal Jutsu.

After Iruka was done berating Naruto for his mistakes, the teacher realized that the class was coming to an end. "Okay everyone, we will now revise the Transformation Jutsu. It will be a big part of the test tomorrow, so remember to practice it," as he said that he glanced at Naruto. "For those who are not sure whether they can use it well enough, make sure to practice harder."

Those words resonated with you, but if you were honest with yourself, sometimes hard work just couldn't do that. The strongest Ninjas have always come from the Strong Ninja Clans, most of the Hokage were from well-established Ninja Clans too, and that said a lot.

Even Minato Namikaze, the 4th Hokage was an exception to that. But he was super talented too, his Chakra reserves were rumored to be massive. There are stories of how he teleported the Nine-Tailed fox away from the village. You didn't know whether that was true, but you knew that the Hokage were strong.

"One by one, form a line and come towards me, demonstrating your Transformation Jutsu," Iruka instructed the students and they formed a line.

You stood at around the end of it as your seat was in the back. The students went and used transformation, you didn't bother too much with it and waited for your turn.

...

When it was your turn, Iruka looked at you and raised his brow. "Shinji?" He waved his hand. "Don't worry, I know you can do it."

You shrugged, seeing that the class was about to end, he needed to test those that he didn't think were good enough to make it and encourage them to study more.

"Transformation Jutsu!!" You heard Naruto yell something behind you, and turning around you saw a naked woman, with only smoke covering the risque parts.

It seemed like Naruto had come up with another stupid Jutsu. But this one you at least understood what it was, and while it seemed silly, you could see that it was useful against... certain kinds of people.

The other students laughed while Iruka got angry at Naruto, with blood spilling out of the teacher's nose. You decided to walk away from this mess and go back to the orphanage.

As you walk along the roads of Konoha, no one pays any attention to you, like always. Even when you entered the orphanage, and went to your room.

Every Academy Student gets their room as soon as they are accepted in the Ninja Academy. Since in their rooms they practiced Jutsu and the village didn't want civilians learning those Jutsu. Especially other orphan children, as they could become irresponsible with them.

Tomorrow will be your last day as an Academy Student. Or at least that was what you assumed. Still, today you could train harder and prepare for tomorrow, or just rest...

□□□□□□□□□□

[Pick one, and write your choice in the comments down below.]

A ○ Rest, and laze about, maybe sleep?

B ○ Train Jutsu

C ○ Train Taijutsu

D ○ Train Jutsu and Taijutsu (Expect lower results than just concentrating on training one.)

＊＊＊＊＊＊＊＊＊＊＊＊＊＊＊＊＊＊＊＊＊

A/N: In the story, you, the reader, will choose how it goes by voting. Be careful though, because there are bad endings, trying to fight someone way above your level will end up with you dead. You have no plot armor, and when it comes to Luck-related events, I just roll dice. If you need more explanations or Shinji's stats, check the Auxiliary Chapters.

Chapter 2: Chapter 2 - Training

[X] Train Jutsu

...

In the end, Shinji decided to train, resting and lazing about just before graduation didn't sound like a good idea to him. After all, his Ninja Career is just beginning, and resting now wasn't a good idea. Unlike many other children, he wasn't too disillusioned with what being a ninja meant.

His Taijutsu was good enough, though his Style was the basics of the academy so most clan kids could defeat him, with a few exceptions. So unless he started training physically, which wouldn't have any effect by tomorrow, Shinji decided to train Ninjutsu. Mostly the Replacement Jutsu, he was sure that even if he became Jonin, that jutsu would be useful. Even life-saving.

But even then, he sat on his bed and contemplated. Training mindlessly wouldn't lead to good results and he knew that. Yet, he tried to think of something, anything that he had missed while he was learning the three basic Jutsu. In his class, he was one of the best ones in using the basic jutsu. He never had an accident when using them, and has known how to use them for years now.

While the Clone and Transformation Jutsu had somewhat limited usages, and when you used them, going through all the hand-signs wasn't a problem. Especially the transformation jutsu, which had only one hand sign.

'Right! Hand Signs!'

Suddenly an idea struck Shinji, and he remembered many times when Iruka -sensei had used only one hand sign for the replacement jutsu.

'How didn't I realize this sooner? It had been right in front of my eyes all along!'

While Shinji wasn't exactly sure how someone could do that, he was determined to at least learn the replacement jutsu to do it faster, because by the speed every Academy Student does it, the jutsu was mostly useless, on par with the other E Rank Jutsu.

Still, he had hours to train and was excited to finally be able to make something of himself. "It should be around six hours until dinner," he muttered and started training religiously.

Finally, the door that had been closed for so long, due to a lack of someone willing to teach him the next level was opened. Shinji knew why the Ninja Clan kids were ahead of him, they had someone to teach them. Even Sasuke, whose whole clan was dead, undoubtedly had a library of the Uchiha Clan Ninjutsu.

But now, he finally found a way to catch up to them.

...

Shinji passed the whole day of training and he didn't know if it was because of finally being decisive in becoming a ninja or maybe he was finally trying something new with the Jutsu he had already learned.

But as he trained, his Replacement Jutsu and Clone Jutsu improved by leaps and bounds. He had finally gotten a new idea and kept training. It made him excited, just like when he learned ninjutsu for the first time.

As the sky turned dark, with only the filing lamp keeping him company, Shinji lept training with an excited smile on his face. Finally, just as he was on the brink of his chakra dropping below 20% and entering the early stages of Chakra Exhaustion.

Poof

Shinji replaced himself with the sheets on his bed. His smile couldn't get any wider. "Well, I tried to replace myself with the chair, but at least this shows that it is possible."

While in the Academy, Shinji worked hard to learn the three basic Jutsu and did so faster than most. But he never thought to try it with fewer hand signs. The Replacement Jutsu might not be ready to be used in combat with fewer hand signs yet, but now he had the key to the door that had been locked to him for quite a while now. Like a child who got a new toy, he felt a burst of joy. He could finally taste the feeling of progress, of getting better.

He was about to continue practicing, but then remembered that he was almost to the brink of chakra exhaustion and stopped. While the Replacement Jutsu didn't use a lot of chakra, training it for hours would have its effect too.

So with excitement bubbling inside of him, Shinji fell asleep.

...

As the next day came about, Shinji woke up early and his chakra was back to normal. His fingers twitched, wanting to train the Replacement Jutsu since the Genin Exams wouldn't start until a couple more hours. But he held that feeling of excitement in, knowing that he had to be at the top of his game when the exam took place.

Looking around his room, Shinji didn't know what to do. So he decided to go to the Academy, even though it was a little early. Better than staying here, where excitement could get the best of him and he might start training.

..

As he walked down the road, a path that he had taken thousands of times, Shinji felt kind of nostalgic, remembering how he used to be at the bottom of the class in physical competitions when he joined. But now he has gotten better, even some of the clan kids, like Ino and Hinata, were below him. Shikamaru too, but the Nara outranked him in the intelligence department, even though their grades were kinda similar.

'I always wondered why Shikamaru never tried harder. He is the smartest one in our class, even though he doesn't show it. I bet he could get the highest test marks if he tried, even a little.'

While most of the class considered Shikamaru a lazy bum, who in the future wouldn't make that good of a ninja. Shinji could see through that demeanor, unlike most of his classmates.

Shinji stopped thinking about others and focused. He couldn't wait until he became a Genin as then he would be able to learn more than just the basic Taijutsu Style that was taught in the academy.

'So many Jutsu...'

When he arrived at the school, it was empty as he expected and except for a couple of janitors, no one else was there. Going to his classroom, he saw that surprisingly, someone else was there. Sasuke Uchiha, the last member of the Uchiha Clan.

Sasuke gave Shinji a side-glance and looked back towards the window. Neither said anything as they just stood there, silently, as he went to his seat in the back. Knowing that the Uchiha wouldn't even reply or just snort in annoyance if he tried to speak.

Shinji had observed how the last Uchiha in Konoha acted and didn't have a favorable opinion of him. First and foremost, Sasuke had no friends, not even the other clan kids. While that wasn't a big deal, even when people

Suddenly, the sliding door to the classroom creaked open and Mizuki -sensei's head popped in. Like always, he had a gentle smile on his face. "Oh? Someone was already here? Sasuke, and… Shinji?"

He noticed how Mizuki said his name, he was a little unsure even though he had been teaching him for years now.

Shinji almost sighed in annoyance. But had to keep it in. The last thing he wanted to do was piss off a teacher on exam day.

This was why he didn't like Mizuki -sensei because while he acted nice and all that, to Shinji, it wasn't a good thing. Iruka worried about his students. While he yelled at them quite a lot, it was because he cared about his students and their futures.

This showed that one of them cared, instead of letting any mistake his students made slide by and not saying anything. Doing that would only be detrimental to their growth.

"You must have been excited about the exam," Mizuki smiled, going towards the desk and taking out a stack of documents, and walking out. Before he did so, he turned towards Shinji and Sasuke.

"I remember when I had my own Graduation Day," he scratched the back of his head nervously, "Hahahaha, those days were quite memorable. I accidentally drank rotten milk that day, and almost failed."

After saying that, he walked off, neither Shinji nor Sasuke said anything. The former folded his arms, he wanted to go train his Replacement Jutsu and felt like time was passing by too slowly.

…

After some time, the quietness in the classroom subsided, as other students came in with a feeling of insecurity and excitement dwelling amongst everyone amongst them. As the class was about to start, even the usually late Naruto had come in time.

Mizuki came in, with a paper in his hand. "I will call your names in alphabetical order. When your name is called, come forward and I will take you to the testing room."

"There is gonna be another room?"

"Oh, God! I thought there would be someone else before me and I could see what the test even was like."

"Wait? Wasn't there a written exam?"

Many of the students started getting a little nervous, but Shinji wasn't amongst them. Having already done some minor 'investigation' if it could be even called that. He just asked the teachers, and some students who failed, and this test wasn't the problem, but the one that came after it was. Though he didn't know exactly what that entailed, as no one spoke about what came after.

"C'mon now everyone, let's calm down," Mizuki remarked, which caused them all to settle. "Let's start, Amara."

...

After a while, a dozen names were called. Right after Shino Aburame, another clan kid that was kind of quiet and was quiet, kind of like Shinji, neither of them ever stood out.

"Shinji, it's your turn," Mizuki waved to him in a friendly manner, patting him on the back as they walked in the hallways. "Don't worry too much. You're one of the students I am confident in passing this exam. You will become a great ninja someday."

Shinji nodded and thanked his teacher, but he guessed that Mizuki -sensei probably told this to everyone already. Entering an empty classroom with only a desk with two chairs where the teachers sat and a chair in the middle of the room. Once he entered, Shinji felt that there was something weird going on, but decided to dismiss this feeling and concentrate on the exam.

Iruka smiled when he saw him. "Shinji, show me the three basic Jutsu."

"Yes, sensei," he went through all of the hand signs and used clones, transformation, and replacement flawlessly.

Shinji didn't try to show how he could somewhat use the Replacement Jutsu with one less hand sign. To him, doing that, sounded like a way to recklessly mess up the exam while trying to look cool.

"Good, you pass," Iruka nodded proudly.

Shinji was excited, even though he was confident he would pass, there was always that doubt in the back of his mind. He picked up a headband, which would serve as head protection too and after thanking his teachers, Shinji walked out with a document in his hand that he had to fill up by tomorrow and come to the Hokage's Office.

Still, equipped with his new headband, Shinji had one place in mind that he had to visit. The library, where an official Ninja and Genin, could learn Ninjutsu. Though it was just scrolls and no one to teach him, it was better than nothing. He knew that his peers that were a part of a Ninja Clan by now knew their clan jutsu and he didn't want to be left behind.

...

After the 'class' was quickly finished, most of the students jumped outside excitedly to their parents.

"Momma! Poppa! I passed!"

"Yes, I did it!"

"I am a Genin, finally!"

Sounds of laughter and happiness filled the academy's courtyard. Shinji wasn't amongst them, not because he wasn't happy, but he was just reminded that he had no parents and no one to celebrate with him.

Still, unlike the usual pang of jealousy in his heart, he was excited to finally learn some new Jutsu. He saw the sad Naruto in a swing who seemed lonely, but Shinji wasn't too worried about that. Having expected something like this already as Naruto had a reputation of a prankster who was a bad student, he slept through most of the classes even when he rarely was there.

He didn't pay too much attention to the sad Naruto. Instead, Shinji decided that today he would treat himself. Every month, he gets a small stipend of money, and he never was a big spender and had been saving it this whole time. But for today, he was going to splurge a little.

Of course for Shinji, splurging money is going to a local Dango Shop and buying some Dango. He didn't have a lot of money saved up, his monthly stipends were that small.

After getting some sweets, he contemplated what to do next, when suddenly he noticed Naruto and Mizuki talking atop a roof.

Now that wouldn't be weird or anything, but Shinji felt like there was something strange as Naruto seemed happy for some reason. Why would a guy who just failed an exam be so happy? He couldn't hear what they were talking about, but it felt suspicious.

_____

[Pick one, and write your choice in the comments down below.]

A ○ Observe what Mizuki and Naruto are up to. Something feels weird.

B ○ Go to the library and learn some more Jutsu. Knowing that they are necessary.

C ○ Go back home and train the Replacement Jutsu. That was a lifesaver. You will keep in mind to go to the library another day.

_____

Relationships:

Naruto 5/10 (Doesn't know you even exist.)

Sasuke 4/10 (He learned that you were in the same classroom today. Consider everyone in the class below him, and not even worth talking to.)

_____

Stats Update:

Ninjutsu: 1 -> 1.1

Replacement (E Rank) [Mastery 50% -> 58%]

Transformation (E Rank) [Mastery 50% -> 51%]

Clone (E Rank) [Mastery 50% -> 55%]

Chapter 3: Chapter 3 - Truth or Lie?

[X] Go back home and train the Replacement Jutsu. That was a lifesaver. You will keep in mind to go to the library another day. (Gained a new Trait: Cautious)

***

Shinji decided that interfering with something like this might develop into a dangerous situation. If a Chunin tried to fight him, he knew that there wasn't anything that he could do against them. The difference between a just-graduating Genin, and Chunin was quite big.

In the future, this might change, but for now, he had to be cautious about what he tried to do.

Shinji walked back to the orphanage, learning that charging into unknown situations could be dangerous.

The old orphanage building greeted him. Unlike what most might think, the orphanage wasn't run down, or that old, since it was built just after the Nine-Tails attacks. But the matron used to be the head of another orphanage, and she was quite old. As he entered inside, the place had children running everywhere, of all ages.

Having lived here for so long, even the smell of the building had become familiar to Shinji. It smelled like home. But even though he was a Ninja, his situation changed little.

After becoming a Genin, his first instinct had been to learn many D Rank Jutsu from the Ninja Library. But he decided against it. After all, even if he learned many Jutsu without mastering them, then it would be the same as learning a thousand useless Jutsu. Just mastering the Replacement Jutsu would be his goal for now, once he had a clear goal.

'I should master the Replacement Jutsu first. Which would be very useful in actual battles as an escape technique. The library isn't going anywhere, and I can go there after this.'

He walked past many children, and like always, he did his best not to stand out amongst the children playing around. Going back to the cramped room that he used to find too tight, Shinji had grown to like the small establishments. Not like he was going to find a new place soon. Just because he became a genin didn't mean his financial situation suddenly changed.

He was still a dirt-poor orphan that would end up becoming a homeless Genin if he moved outside of the orphanage.

knock *knock* *knock*

Just as he was about to train when he heard three soft knocks on the door, after opening it, outside stood an old woman with a crouched back, white hair, and a gentle grandmotherly look on her face as she gazed at him. "It feels like you're growing so fast nowadays. I still remember the days you were just a small babe..."

..

The old woman continued talking for a dozen minutes. Shinji didn't interrupt her. Because this gentle-looking grandma was the matron of this place, and getting on her bad side wasn't something he wanted to do.

Also, there were some rumors that she might have been a ninja. Some say that she was a Legendary Ninja of the past who killed a hundred enemy shinobi.

Shinji wasn't sure about that, as rumors were usually blown out of proportion. But he wasn't against the idea either, as raising the orphans of the village was a job that had to be given to someone trustworthy to not sell kids into the back market.

Killing a thousand ninja? Shinji believed that wasn't true. Since if it was true, someone of her stature would be too useful to let go. Instead, she should teach the younger generation.

hic *hic* "Shinji," the old matron now had tears in her eyes. "Never forget that this will always be your home. If anything happens, you can always come back here."

"Uhhh, okay," he nodded awkwardly, patting the matron on the back to console her. Truly, Shinji didn't have any attachments to this place. When growing up, he didn't have any friends. Few orphans went to the academy, and those who did had dropped out by now. At least, those that were from the same orphanage had dropped out. "Yes, of course. I will always remember this place."

He tried to smile and make the atmosphere a little more somber. "Also, it's not like I am going away any time soon."

The matron wiped the tears off her eyes with a pearly white clean napkin. "A Genin is calling you to the door and has come to notify you that you'll be moving into a Ninja Dormitory. You know, I hope Shinobi can be with practicing potentially dangerous Jutsu and rigging their residences, can't have them living just anywhere. But still!! Shinji! If you don't wanna go, just tell me!"

'Actually, I wanna go as fast as I can. It sounds like a good place and it's probably bigger than this and hopefully, there is a toilet I don't have to share with everyone else.' Thought Shinji, but decided not to voice out his opinions due to not wanting to upset the matron.

Having a bigger place to stay would help with his training, too. "Well, I am going to meet the Genin that came here and see what they want."

Shinji dodged the matron and went towards the door. He didn't hate the woman and even liked her, as she never treated him unfairly. But he knew that if he kept her company as she cried, he would be stuck there for hours. He had seen that scene twice when previous orphanage members moved away.

After going outside, he saw it was a short-haired man with a stubble of facial hair on his chin. He only had a headband and no Chunin jacket, so Shinji assumed that the man must truly be a genin. Some Jonin didn't need to wear the flat jacket when outside, but he doubted it was important to be escorted by a Jonin. "Hello," Shinji greeted the man cordially. "Can I help you?"

"Yeah," the genin nodded. "Gather your stuff, and I will show you your new living quarters."

Shinji almost jumped up in excitement. He didn't know that there was housing provided for the ninja. But he knew that if he played his cards right, not only would he have a new place to stay, but also the place where he would train, sleep, and study.

Going back to his room, or now ex-room, Shinji hugged the matron, the feeling of happiness from finally moving away still was within him. "Matron, thanks for everything over the years. When I have breaks, I might come and visit sometimes. By then, I hope my name will be known."

While his words came from the happiness that he felt from getting a new place, there was also some genuine emotion in them. He truly was grateful for the Metreon he got. He never went to sleep hungry, and no one from the orphanage ever bothered or bullied him.

The matron just smiled at him sadly. "Oh well, it wouldn't feel right for an old woman like me with one foot in the grave to keep you from your dreams."

"Matron, stay alive a little longer," Shinji smiled at her. "Without you, many people would be sad. Me included."

She looked at the ground as if contemplating something. But she came out of her deep, reminiscing thoughts, and smacked Shinji in the back lightly. "Go now, before I regret my decision, and keep you here."

He chuckled and ran off with only a small bag over his shoulder. Shinji had little belongings, as even the sheets he used to sleep in were the orphanage's property. Well, technically, the clothes on his back didn't belong to him either, but he would not run through Konoha naked.

The genin outside waved at him to follow and silently started walking away. Shinji did so without saying much at first, but not long after, he asked. "So, do we get to keep the apartments after moving in?"

He couldn't see how that would make sense from a village economical standpoint. Shinji was sure that Konoha had at least 6000 Genin. Though the number of Ninjas in any Hidden Village is undisclosed, as that would give information to the enemy that could be used against them.

"No, after five years, if you haven't become a Chunin then you'll have to start paying rent," answered the Genin visually, getting an annoyed look. Which made Shinji guess that he probably had some difficulties with a similar situation in the past.

But now Shinji understood why Konoha gave away free apartments to the Genins. Not only was it to be used as an enticement, for the Genin to take the Chunin exam so the apartment could stay free. But even the Genin, after years of living there, would develop a sense of home, get to know their neighbors, maybe even form friendships in the area. Those factors and many others combined cause them to pay rent, no matter how high the price was.

'As expected, whoever is in charge of these decisions, made an excellent system on how to handle these things. Better be careful, so I don't end in debt, or sign a contract with a loophole in it.'

People always say that ninjas have high wages. Even low-ranking missions paid a lot. At least that was what Shinji heard, and he wasn't sure of the facts on the matter.

...

Neither of them said much, and they arrived at Shinji's new apartment. It was in a normal-looking neighborhood. There were a lot of shops nearby too.

The genin handed him the keys to the apartment and walked away, going to do his job. "See you around... hopefully you don't die too soon."

Shinji ignored the latter part of his words. "This apartment building should be filled with Ninja, but looks so normal from the outside."

Opening the front door, the first thing that caught Shinji's eyes was the spacious living room. While the furniture had a dull decoration, he saw a bed in the middle of the living room. To the right was a bathroom, and at the end sat a small balcony. The living space here was infinitely better than the cramped room in the orphanage.

Putting his bag down, which only had some notebooks, a change of clothes, and some pens. So nothing really special. Still, Shinji knew these things were his, and would not leave his last possessions behind.

Checking out the room, there was a note on the dining table. It was a list of rules and what you're allowed to do. Though as Shinji read along, it was mostly a list of what not to do when you booby trap the room.

'Not using explosive tags that could destroy the neighbors' room, you must pay for damage done by your traps.'

The list was quite detailed, and while there wasn't a limit on the lethality of the traps. Property destruction and traps that annoy the neighbors were forbidden.

"It's like they expect me to build traps already?" Muttered Shinji, as he looked towards the balcony and another window. While he had some theoretical knowledge of traps, he never put them into practice before. Also, who would even want to harm an average Genin like him? It wasn't like he had some special talent or secret information about anything.

Still, he would worry about traps later. Especially since there were many ninjas in this building, and there might even be some Jonin. They would notice intruders before Shinji. So for now, trapping his room wasn't something he saw as being needed, though he might later.

Then he laid down on his soft bed, feeling the texture of the sheets and giggling. "It's soft."

After that small, momentary enjoyment, he immediately got up and started training his Replacement Jutsu. It felt like soon he could use it with one less hand sign. Also, the familiarity of using the Replacement Jutsu has made him able to go through the hand signs faster than before.

"Still, I need to improve faster," but this did not satisfy Shinji with just so much progress. Now that he had gotten a taste, he wanted more. He wanted to be better than this, and wasn't satisfied at all.

...

His training continued until night came about. Like yesterday, he also brought his chakra down to a level where he knew it would be filled up during the next day.

So by night, he learned how to use the Replacement Jutsu with one less hand sign and it made a big difference. While the chakra consumption was a little bigger when using fewer hand signs. But the difference wasn't anything to worry about.

Sitting on his dining room table, Shinji stared at a note in front of him. It was the registration paper, where he had stapled a photo of himself on, and there were things that one needed to write. Like name, hobbies, and date of birth.

He thought about what his hobbies were, and there wasn't anything he liked. Lying in the village didn't sound like a good idea either, especially for such small things.

But Shinji remembered recently what he had been doing.

_____

[Pick one, and write your choice in the comments down below.]

A ○ Write the truth. You've shown an interest in Jutsu, and how far you can push them. So that should qualify as a hobby.

B ○ Lie, and write something that sounds. (Was it a good idea to lie about something this small? Would someone investigate and figure it out?)

C ○ Write nothing in the hobbies section. (This might seem like you have something to hide.)

_____

Stats Update:

Replacement (E Rank) [Mastery 58% -> 63%]

Hand Seals: 1 -> 1.1

[Cautious] (New Trait!)

Shinji can generally tell when a situation is likely to develop in a dangerous direction. He isn't reckless and is less likely to get caught by surprise during a sneak attack.

Sometimes it will give hints of which options might be dangerous to take. (This time the hints are in brackets, to make them more noticeable what I mean. But they won't be anymore.)

The warnings are just what Shinji perceives as dangerous, so they might not always be true.

_____

Relationships:

Old Orphanage Matron 7/10 (Though you weren't the most outgoing or loving kid around. She cares for every child in the orphanage.)

Chapter 4: Chapter 4 - Genin Team, and Jonin Teacher

[X] Write the truth. You've shown an interest in Jutsu, and how far you can push them. So that should qualify as a hobby.

…

Lying isn't a smart thing to do in this situation. He was surrounded by ninjas in the apartment building, and any of them could notice his hobbies. Ninjas were known for many things, and any competent ninja would pay attention to details like this. Or just be nosy as hell.

With that in mind, he wrote down on his hobbies tab: Studying Jutsu and seeing their limits, and how far I can push them.

'That should be good enough, and for some reason, anyone decides to investigate. They will see that it was the truth.'

Shinji was being cautious, but he knew that the village had nothing against him. He also understood that he was weak, and his mistakes won't be forgiven. There was no great clan to support him either.

The chances of an investigation were small. But why take the risk at all?

…

As the morning sun hit his face, Shinji immediately woke up. His body felt like jelly as he laid down on the soft mattress. This night had been one of the best he had ever had. The mass-produced, overused mattresses in the orphanage didn't even compare to it. "After making some money, I should spoil myself a little."

He put on his usual clothes and walked out with a small but gleeful smile on his face. He had some money on hand and went to the nearby shop, and bought some ninja tools. Kunai, shuriken, bandages, and even ninja wire.

'As expected, there are a lot of ninja tool shops in their neighborhood too.' Shinji paid attention to the smaller details, observing everyone and trying to see how the economy around here worked. "The prices were cheaper than I thought."

…

When he arrived at the Hokage's building, Shinji had his paper in hand and walked towards the receptionist at the entrance. "Excuse me, I am here to deliver my ID paper. Where do I need to go?"

The receptionist was a black-haired woman, with glasses and dark eyes. She seemed to exude a strict atmosphere. "Go to that room, it has Genin Counseling written on it."

He nodded and went towards the room, and once he opened the door, he saw the Hokage, Hiruzen Sarutobi sitting at a wide table. With two Chunin by his side, helping him with paperwork.

"Oh, Shinji, welcome," the Hogake had a grandfatherly smile on his face. Shinji didn't know exactly how to act, because while he had seen the Hokage from far away he never talked to the man directly. The old man pointed towards a single stool in the middle of the room.

"Give me the paper, and I will ask a couple of questions," his grandfatherly smile seemed to go up a level. "Don't worry, there is no need to be nervous. Think of this as more of a casual conversation."

Shinji nodded. "Thanks, Hokage -sama."

He respectfully bowed his head a little and went to sit down. Hiruzen started reading his ID and hummed affirmingly, reassuring Shinji that there wasn't anything wrong with his papers. "Oh? Studying Jutsu? And seeing their limits?"

"Ah, yes," Shinji nodded. "I have recently realized that you can use fewer hand signs in a Jutsu. So I have been repeating training with that and trying to take away hand signs. I can now use the Replacement Jutsu with four hand signs."

"Ohh~" the Hokage had an impressed look in his eyes. "That's quite impressive. Usually, only during Chunins realize something like that."

Hiruzen then got up and walked towards Shinji, smiling and giving him a book. He was confused at first and read the title. " Detailed explanation of chakra and hand seals," it sounded like quite an important book and Shinji smiled. He didn't know how rare this book was, but he still thanked the Hokage. "Thank you."

But the old man only riffles his hair and says, "Don't worry about it. I just see a lot of potential in you, and this is my investment in someone that I see has a bright future. Continue to work hard and I am sure you will become an amazing Ninja."

Not knowing what to make of this, Shinji just stood there, looking at the book curiously. Suddenly, the door opened once again, and this time it was someone familiar that came in. His yellow-blonde hair, and the 'I am here' orange jumpsuit made it clear that this was undoubtedly Naruto, without even needing to look at his face.

"Gramps, I retook the photo," Naruto stated with the ID paper in his hands. He seemed annoyed at having to do such a thing. "Tch, the last photo was cooler though."

"Hahahaha," Hiruzen had a hearty laugh at Naruto's behavior. "It was a ridiculous photo, no one would ever recognize who you even were. By the way, do you know Shinji?" the Hokage pointed at him.

"Shinji?" Naruto tilted his head in confusion and inspected him. "He looks kinda familiar…"

Hiruzen glanced at the energetic blonde with a dull look. "He has been one of your classmates for over four years now."

"He has!!" Naruto was shocked as if he had just gotten a grand reveal. "Wow, I never knew," he smiled, sheepishly rubbing the back of his head. He didn't seem to notice that if he had said those words to anyone else, they would have been mad. "Nice to meet you."

Naruto extended his hand, and Shinji shook his hand and smiled back. "Nice to meet you too Naruto," and after saying that he walked out, knowing that Naruto had to complete his questions too. "Hokage -sama, thank you for everything. Also, hope you have a good day too, Naruto."

As he walked out, Shinji noticed a small kid badly hidden by holding up a sheet that looked like the wall behind him. He decided to ignore the weird kid and just walked out.

Still, there was one thing that surprised him, though he didn't say anything about it to the Hokage.

'How did Naruto pass? I know for a fact that he failed the exam. But then again, he did call the Hokage, gramps. So it's probably some kind of power abuse and he had Naruto pass the Genin exam. Oh well, I am not going to complain.'

Looking at the book in his hand, Shinji knew that Naruto wasn't the only one the Hokage showed favoritism towards. As he had also received a book, and he didn't know the full details of the situation yet. But he had never heard of a student who failed the genin exam suddenly becoming a genin before the time for the next exam came around.

...

Going back to his new apartment, Shinji was careful to keep an eye out for his neighbors, he would like to get to know them. But there was no one outside yet. He went to his residence which still had the smell of a new apartment. Probably the smell of paint and new furniture.

Shinji went to his bed, and with the book, in his hand, he slumped onto the warm, soft, and tender bed. Since this was a book given to him by the Hokage, he knew that it wasn't anything normal or that he would find it in the genin library. Opening it, the first page immediately made it clear what Rank of Shinobi this book was.

"For Jonin?" Shinji was baffled, knowing that he wasn't special enough for the Hokage to have so much trust in him. "Heh, I guess even the Hokage can make mistakes. But still, it would be a shame to not at least try."

For the moment, Shinji wanted to train the Replacement Jutsu until he could use it with one hand sign only. But this book would help him achieve that faster, as he needed an outside perspective on his work.

Unlike what he expected, Shinji wasn't baffled by the first pages and easily understood them. "Woah! You can use another person's hand to make a hand sign?!"

...

It took Shinji only a couple of hours to read the thousands of words and descriptions in the book. Now he knew why Hiruzen was called 'The Professor' within the book. There were many things that Shinji hadn't even thought of and would have encountered problems with in the future. It gave him a whole new meaning in hand signs, before when he was trying to lessen the hand signs in the Replacement Jutsu he was going through every detail in trial and error.

But now, this book had many people who had gone through similar experiences and at the end of the book there were descriptions from the Second Hokage at how he went to using the Water Dragon Jutsu from forty-four hand signs to five and there were some descriptions in the end that there was a way to go to only four hand signs.

"Oy, oy, oy, this isn't funny. This guy went from over forty hand signs of an A-Rank Jutsu to a measly four," Shinji was amazed, while in the Academy they learned how Tobirama Senju was known for his Water Style Jutsu. He never imagined it was at this level. "Fuck," he unconsciously swore. "Here I am having trouble with a simple E Rank Jutsu."

...

At first, Shinji felt crushed by the difference in raw talent. But not long after his gaze sharpened, and a smile came to his face. He opened the book again, and this time it was during the basic parts. "I will need to increase Chakra Control at the later stages of learning how to use this Jutsu without hand seals. Tobirama, thank you for being such a goddamn genius because I will reap the fruits of your labor and effort that you put in this book."

He didn't know why Hiruzen decided to give him such a book because even though the writer's name wasn't stated directly, he could guess who wrote this. Tobirama Senju, the 2nd Hokage, seemed to have been a genius that nowadays doesn't exist.

...

As night came about, Shinji had been easily able to use the replacement Jutsu with only three hand seals now, two down from the original five. He could use it with two too, but with that, the replacement was a little wobbly and not battle-ready.

The fewer hand signs he had to use, the harder it was supposed to get. But following the instructions in the book, it seemed to become way easier.

Was this what it felt like to be a genius?

The book had offered Shinji a way to look into the Author's mindset and thought process. Slowly, but surely, he grew to admire Tobirama's mastery of Chakra and Jutsu. In just one night, Shinji had made progress that would have taken months. No, maybe even years. By reading this book, not only had he skipped a major part of the trial and error process, but his understanding of Ninjutsu, Hand Seals, and Chakra, in general, had changed.

'Will I be able to be as good as him one day?' he wondered while turning off the light in his room and tucking himself under the warm bed sheets. 'A Hokage, I do not care enough about the position that much. As it sounds like I would have to deal with a mountain of paperwork every day. But...'

Solely, while thinking such thoughts, he drifted into sleep. Unknowingly, ambition had started to take root in Shinji's mind. Whether it would sprout into something more, only time will tell.

...

The next day, within the academy grounds, Shinji walked towards his class with a book in his hand. It wasn't the book the Hokage gave him, as he didn't want anyone to get a hold of that content. Early this morning he had bought a weak storage scroll, which wiped his savings away. But he also put that scroll in a small metal box in his pocket.

Better be safe than sorry. Also now he had the book with him at all times and that would be helpful if he wanted to read it in his free time. After memorizing the contents in the book, he planned to burn it. But memorizing all that would take at least a week.

As he opened the door to his classroom, a strange sight greeted Shinji. He wondered if this was some kind of Genjutsu. Naruto and Sasuke were kissing, while the whole class was looking at them. "Huh, never knew they swung that way."

It didn't take long for the banshee-... Sakura to beat up Naruto, yelling something about him taking Sasuke's first kiss.

Shinji dodged out of this situation, not wanting to get involved, and went to the back of the classroom. Observing the drama from afar, which was an enjoyable distance.

Shikamaru, who was closer to the drama, got up and sat down next to Shinji. "They're too troublesome. Can't even let a guy sleep in peace."

"For me, it's kinda entertaining," Shinji added jokingly. "Do you think Ino will get in there and fight with Sakura?"

"Nah, she won't," the lazy guy muttered, and then pointed towards where Ino sat. She peered at Sakura with a deadly gaze, and grinded her teeth in rage. But she didn't move. Feeling Shinji's curious side-glance, Shikamaru explained. "Uncle has been quite hard on her recently. The dieting, bad grades and overall failure as a Ninja enraged uncle Inoichi. She is supposed to be the future Clan Head. So the situation is quite complicated, and the family elders have caught on with what was happening."

"You sure it's okay to tell me this?" Shinji inquired, not wanting to be in possession of any sensitive information. Because that would be the same as a time-bomb, because people would eventually start looking for it.

Shikamaru shrugged. "Anyone who doesn't need to know, already knows this."

'That sounds like something too troublesome. I guess even being a clan member, if you're complacent, then the political side of the clan will sink their claws in like hungry wolves.'

Looking at the pitiful sight of Naruto, Shinji couldn't help but sigh. "I don't understand why he even has a crush on someone like Sakura? Her personality is terrible. If we're going by looks-only the Ino would be better."

yawn "Maybe he likes getting beat up. Some people are really into that. He probably is only showing the early symptoms for now."

"Who knows, maybe he is under a Genjutsu?" Shinji chuckled, which made the Nara heir crack a small smile.

"Probably brain damage from all the hits she keeps giving him. Or that might be the trigger for the Genjutsu."

..

Shinji and Shikamaru surprisingly got along quite well. Like gossiping housewives they kept bad-mouthing everyone noteworthy in the class. The kiss between Naruto and Sasuke though was the main subject of most of the discussion.

But their ridiculous theories of Naruto being a mastermind and orchestrating the kiss because he was in love with Sasuke all along, stopped. Iruka came in, and he had a large notebook in his hands. "Okay everyone, settle down. Today we have the team placements, and we don't have too much time to discuss these as you'll have to get to know your teammates and Jonin teacher."

..

"Team 7, Naruto Uzumaki, Sakura Haruno, and Sasuke Uchiha," Iruka stated. "Your Jonin teacher will be Kakashi Hatake."

Shinji chuckled at the reactions from team seven. In the end, the last team to be called was his. But now he had caught on what was happening and how the team placements were made, it was either due to their grades, or specialty.

"Team 13, Shinji, Kota Harada, Sayuri. Your Jonin teacher will be Yamato," after saying that, Iruka closed the book and pointed towards the door. "Now each of your Jonin teachers will come and take you after the lunch break."

Hearing that, Shinji immediately got up and said goodbye to Shikamaru. "See you later. Gotta go and get to know my teammates."

"Yeah, yeah, now I have to deal with Ino," he sighed and got up, going to help Choji who was holding back the blonde Yamanaka, as she wanted to charge at Sakura for being so lucky.

Trying to find his teammates, it didn't take long for Shinji to find them. Kota was a young man, with a bigger than average build, for his age and he had brown hair, and sunken brown eyes. Don't let his size lie to you, because while Kota was good in taijutsu and one of the best amongst the civilians, Shinji had spared against him in class a couple of times and won all three times they fought.

His other teammate was Sayuri, since she had no last name Shinji assumed that she was likely an orphan just like himself. Though from another orphanage. She had long dark hair, pale white skin, and blue eyes. Shinji tried to remember what she was good at, but couldn't come up with anything. At least she wasn't like Sakura and Ino who always seemed to yell annoyingly when Sasuke was around.

'As a team we need to get familiar with each other, and build some trust.' Shinji viewed this as a necessity. The last thing he wanted was for his teammates to leave him behind in a sticky situation. This wouldn't be that weird to happen, since they weren't friends before this.

Shinji waved at both of them, with a friendly smile on his face. "Kota, Sayuri, we are a team now. Let's get along."

Since they had spent four years in the same class, unless your name was Naruto, you should remember your classmates. So they too knew of Shinji.

Kota took the initiative and smiled back, walking towards Shinji and putting an arm behind his neck in a friendly. "Hell yeah! Let's become the best team here!"

"Yes..." Sayuri answered simply. She didn't seem like the kind to be open with other people, and kind of introverted.

Shinji saw that, and decided to not push the girl. So he took out the lunch he had brought along and showed them. "How about we go and get lunch together."

Kota was quick to agree, but Sayuri looked down in embarrassment. Shinji caught on quickly and understood what was happening. "Kota, how about you go and buy lunch while I and Sayuri will wait for you on the roof."

He nodded and excitedly ran off. Syauri still seemed embarrassed as the class emptied out, with everyone going out to eat lunch with their friends or new teammates. Only they were left behind, and Shinji opens his lunch box and offers some to her. "Did you forget to make lunch for yourself?"

She noods, with an embarrassed blush adorning her face. Though Shinji could guess many things why she forgot, probably because she might not be used to eating lunch in school. Some orphanages were worse than the one he grew up in, and that was why he is grateful to his matron.

"C'mon, let's go to the roof, I made this lunch to eat with my new teammates anyway," he lied, but decided to do so as to not embarrass Sayuri. He knew how orphans felt in her position, he had been there too. "With Kota getting his own lunch, we have a feast."

As they walk to the roof, Sayuri doesn't say much. But Shinji keeps the conversation going. "Hopefully our Jonin sensei is a good one, and actually teaches us some useful jutsu."

"Yes," he nodded, a small smile adorning her face. Sayuri seemed to contemplate something, but Shinji couldn't see what she was thinking. Turning towards him, as they stood on the roof, staring down at the ground below them, she offered him a hand.

"Shinji, I hope that we will be a good team," she muttered awkwardly. "Uhhh... if you need anything, don't be afraid to ask."

He nodded, and while Shinji understood her, they were in a somewhat similar situation. So there was an understanding between them. But the last thing he wanted was to have a dead-weight teammate.

Not remembering much about Sayuri's academy record, he inquired. "By the way, what were your grades in the academy? As for me, my written exam scores were good. But that isn't so important now. Also, I am better than average at the Replacement Jutsu."

Shinji was being a little reserved here, but he didn't want to come out as arrogant. "Also, if you need any help in training Jutsu, I can help you. Though the Jonin teacher would do better at training us, it's still better to be a little transparent with the team. We don't want secrets between us."

Of course, he wasn't going to tell them everything. But for now, Shinji needed his team's trust. Of course, such a thing couldn't be built in a day, but consistently showing that you trust each other would help.

"I was good in biology, and can spot poisonous plants, and what would be edible in a forest," she added helpfully.

Shinji smiled, as to not discourage her, but he too knew about edible plants and all that. But decided to keep his mouth shut about it. "Oh? Then that will be useful when we camp."

..

Not long after that, Kota joined them, though by then both Shinji and Sayuri had eaten their lunch.

"Ahh~ you guys went ahead without me," he chuckled, not taking offense to it, sitting down and enjoying his lunch.

"What do you guys wanna do in the future?" Asked Shinji, trying to inquire what they were after.

"Meh, become a Jonin," Kaido admitted without missing a beat. "My parents are always working so hard, and did everything they could to put me in the Academy. But after I become a Jonin, they won't have to work anymore."

"That's an admirable goal," Sayuri smiled, understanding where he was coming from. "As for me, I want to just be a Chunin, earn enough money, and live a good life. Also there aren't a lot of options for me, as I don't know how to do anything else."

Shinji was about to tell them his goals too when the bell rang, signaling them that they had to go back to Class. "Well, let's not annoy our Jonin teacher and make him have to wait."

After going back to Class, the students had all sat down, and Team 13 all sat down on the same desk. While it wasn't the best team, or the one with the most potential in the class, Shinji was confident that they got along quite well and understood each other.

"Team 8, come with me," suddenly a beautiful woman came in, she had red eyes, dark hair and pale skin. Her uniform was a little strange as it seemed like she was wearing bandages. "I am Kurenai Yuhi and will be your Jonin teacher."

One by one Jonin came in to pick their teams, and Shinji felt himself growing nervous. Escape Team 7, every other Jonin seemed to already be here. Still, many thoughts went through his mind, would his teacher be good? Would he teach them? Or maybe he will drop them because they're too bothersome?

That was when a man wearing a Jonin uniform came in, just like many of the teachers before. He has short brown hair and black, almond-shaped eyes. His gaze settled on Team 13, and Shinji noticed that the new Jonin -sensei seemed to stare at him a second later than the rest of his teammates.

"Team 13, you're with me," he silently signaled for them to come, and they followed. As they walked out of the class, the teacher introduced himself. "My name is Yamato, and I will be your Jonin -sensei if you're able to pass my test."

All three members of team 13, Shinji included, nodded rigidly and didn't ask any questions as their teacher seemed to be quite strict. Seeing this, Yamato smiled at them, and the unapproachable atmosphere around him changed. "Well, we will worry about the test tomorrow, and instead, today we will get to know each other."

...

Yamato ended up taking his team to a very well known, and expensive barbeque restaurant that belonged to the Akimichi Clan. Looking at the menu prices made Shinji pale, the money he had previously saved before was nothing in comparison to this.

"Seeing their expressions, Yamato couldn't hold back, "Hahahaha," and laughed. "Don't worry and pick whatever you want."

Shinji was the first one to come to his senses and pointed to the most expensive items. Yamato shrugged, as if that amount of money was nothing to him. It made Shinji go green with greed, he wanted that kind of money too.

"Anway," Yamato pulled them back to reality as the water went to get their orders. "How about we get to know each other? Tell me your names and where do you see yourself in five years?"

The genin thought about their answers, and Yamato decided to be a little more forthcoming. "Well, I will start by myself, and show you how it's done. My name is Yamato, a certified Jonin of Konoha, and in five years I see myself raising three amazing ninjas and helping them blossom to their full potential."

"How about you go next, big guy," he pointed at Kota.

Taking a deep breath, Kota got rid of his nerves. "My name is Kota Harada, and in five years, I see myself being a chunin."

"Hmmm," Yamato seemed to contemplate and then pointed at Sayuri as his elbows leaned on the table. "What about you?"

"M -My name is Sayuri, and in five years I want to have some money saved, a boyfriend, and hopefully be a chunin," she answered with a blushing face.

'Hopefully she isn't a Sasuke fan-girl, having a Sakura in our team sounds like a nightmare waiting to happen.'

With those thoughts in mind, Shinji was the last to answer and looked at his Jonin sensei confidently. "In five years,

———————————————

[Pick one, and write your choice in the comments down below.]

A ○ "I want to be a Jonin of Konoha..."

B ○ "I see myself walking down the road of the Second Hokage, and eventually surpassing him..."

C ○ "I want to master at least 100 Jutsu and be able to use them without hand signs..."

D ○ "I want to be known as an S Rank Ninja..."

E ○ "I want to be just like the Second Hokage..."

————

Author Note:

Join discord where I post the dice rolls of the chapter and their effects. Since there are quite a lot of them and I don't wanna fill the chapter with dice roll numbers.

Discord:

https://discord.gg/wbwRTqd7jr

Also, Shinji had some good dice rolls in this chap. Pretty lucky of him.

————

Status Update:

Replacement (E Rank) [Mastery 63% -> 77%]

Ninjutsu: 1.1 -> 1.7

Intelligence: 3 -> 3.2

Hand Seals: 1.1 -> 1.6

Chakra: 2 -> 2.1

————

Relationships:

Naruto 5/10 (He now knows Shinji exists.)

Hiruzen Sarutobi 7/10 (He is impressed by Shinji, and sees a visage of someone in the past on him.)

Shikamaru 6/10 (He thinks that Shinji is fun to be around.)

Kota 6/10 (Shinji seems like an okay teammate to have.)

Sayuri 7/10 (She is grateful to Shinji for saving her from an embarrassing situation..)

Chapter 5: Chapter 5 - Ambition

[B] "I see myself walking down the road of the Second Hokage, and eventually surpassing him..." (New Trait: Crazily Ambitious)

.....

Shinji thought about the answer and in the end, muttered. "I see myself walking down the road of the Second Hokage, and eventually surpassing him..."

His teammates were shocked at such a revelation, and it showed in their faces. Yamato on the other hand, while seeming surprised, had a small smile on his face.

"I know it might sound arrogant for an orphan like me to aim so high," Shinji added, knowing how his dream might sound to the others. "But I want to truly be one of the strongest ninjas to ever walk this earth," he clenched his fist, peering at the burning barbeque flame. "One life, that's all I have, and will ever have. Just one chance to achieve something, and I don't want to settle for something mediocre."

Kota had a strange look in his eyes as he heard Shinji's words, suddenly, a huge grin adorned his face. At first, when Shinji saw this, he frowned, thinking that he was about to be ridiculed.

"Hell yeah!" but instead he was greeted by a cheer from his teammate. "You're right. Shinji, my dream for the future was to be a simple Jonin. But you woke me up, I only have one life, so instead, I will become an S Rank Ninja whose name will be spoken throughout the five nations," he then glanced back at Yamato, who had a face full of smiles. "Sensei, I change my answer, in the next five years I need to be at least a Jonin, or I will never be able to become an S Rank Ninja."

Sayuri was a little meeker, but she still smiled at her teammates. "Yes, and I wi-... will be there to help you both."

"Well, it seems like as your Jonin teacher, I will have to try hard and make sure to pave the road to your dreams," Yamato chuckled, he seemed happier than when they had initially met. He no longer had that smile which was there just to be polite. Now, he seemed genuinely happy. "Then I hope you will do well in tomorrow's final genin test. You'll have to fight me, so come prepared. Be at the twenty-first training ground before seven in the morning."

...

The rest of the dining went extremely well and Shinji was happy to have these teammates. While they might not be the most talented out there, like Sasuke, he would still choose his current teammates over the last Uchiha any day.

When he went back home, Shinji smiled at his clean apartment and he didn't even go to lie down in bed and started going through hand signs, trying to regulate his Chakra flow so he can do the Replacement Jutsu with one less hand seal. By now progress should be at a snail's pace, and it was true, Shinji was feeling the burden of training.

...

Even as night came about, the progress he made was minuscule compared to yesterday.

'Maybe I should just go to bed and try tomorrow.' He thought as he was getting a little tired, and training without progress was disheartening. But then he remembered his goal, and the fire in his eyes blossomed like a flower. "No fucking way! I am not stopping now, if I can't master an E Rank Jutsu, how the hell can I dream of mastering those of A and S Rank!

Even his chakra seemed to respond to his emotions as it burst out explosively, taking a deep breath, he calmed himself and went through the three hand-seals in less than a second. His body had memorized the hand signs for the Replacement Jutsu to its core and could do them in his sleep.

poof

He replaced himself with a chair at the corner of the room, and then he did it again, with the same chair. But this time with two hand seals, and only to his hard-headedness, he was able to replace himself with the same chair.

This time, he perfectly did it, but Shinji didn't celebrate as this could have just been a fluke. He went through the hand seals again and this time replaced himself with another chair. Within an instant, he changed positions, and the familiar feeling of initial disorientation from changing places was still there. But by now, he wasn't bothered by it, and a huge smile appeared on his face. "Seems like my efforts paid off. Never rest in the middle of something, rest at the end."

He went and slumped on the bed, and sleep came to him easily as he was tired from another night of training.

...

As morning came about, within training ground twenty-one, Shinji was there early, when he noticed one of his teammates coming.

"Did you sleep well?" asked Kota, with his usual smile, he rushed closer and put an arm around Shinji. "By the way, let's work together today and use me as bait if you have to. Back in the academy, you were better at Taijutsu, but I can take a beating. So we could use that as a chance. I thought of this plan all night, what do you think about it?"

'That was a plan? What about the details? At best that was an idea, and even then not a fully flagged one.' Shinji made sure to keep his thoughts to himself, as he knew saying them out loud would sound condescending. 'How do I say this more nicely?'

"Your idea is good," he started, choosing his next words carefully. "But we need to have a signal or something that only we know about. It doesn't have to be something complicated, a nod will do."

"Yes, that will work. When Yamato -sensei is attacking me, don't save me, but use that moment to attack him."

"What are you guys talking about?" Sayuri's voice sounded out as she arrived early too. She seemed more comfortable than usual.

Kota gave her an excited thumbs up. "We're coming up with some plans. I'm going to be the bait while Shinji will be the main attacker, my taijutsu sucks, but his is pretty good."

While his teammate kept explaining the plan in detail, Shinji knew that his taijutsu wasn't likely to do anything or even match up against an opponent at Yamato's level. The taijutsu style taught in the academy is basic and while it is generally good at defending, attacking, and even dodging, it has no specialty. It's good as a basic exercise that would allow anyone to learn another style after they became a genin. But against even a Chunin, it was bound to be ineffective.

While Shinji didn't have a clear grasp of what a Jonin was able to do, the book written by Tobirama Senju somewhat gave him a hint. Still, he decided to see how the battle would go, and decide then.

That was when Shinji realized something. 'If our chances of winning against a Jonin are almost nonexistent. Then what did Yamato -sensei want to see from us? What're the criteria to pass the test?'

His thoughts were interrupted, as suddenly the wind around them seemed to pick up as in a swirl of leaves, Yamato appeared, with a serious look on his face. Kota waved and went to greet him. "Hey, Ya-"

Fwish!

But he couldn't finish whatever he was about to say, as Yamato's foot sunk into his stomach and Kota's eyes widened, saliva spewed out of his mouth.

Baaam!!

He crashed into a tree and smashed it to pieces due to the force behind the attack. Within the next split second, Sayuri suffered the same, with a kick pushing her into the forest.

Yamato turned and his eyes were cold, emotionless, and it made a cold chill crawl up Shinji's spine. "Everyone has a plan until they get beaten to a pulp," the jonin muttered in an almost whisper-like voice.

Fwish!

The only thing Shinji felt was the wind before the attack came as his eyes couldn't even see the attack, but he was able to instinctively analyze where Yamato had attacked his two teammates previously. Both in the stomach, so he crossed his arms, just barely in time to stop a devastating kick.

Shinji felt his arms creak, as if they were about to be broken, he was pushed back but was able to stop himself from smashing into a tree by digging his feet on the ground and leaving a trail into the earth as he was pushed back.

"Impressive," stated Yamato, simply. "You were able to read my movements, and within a split second came to the conclusion where I am likely to attack."

'Yeah, except you make it sound easy sensei. My body knew what to do before my mind even caught up. Also, this won't work a second time.'

Shinji's arms shook uncontrollably as they slumped to the side, still shaking, a piercing pain ran through them. The hit had been devastating.

"Can you guess where I will attack this time again? Prove to me that it wasn't a fluke."

'But it was a fluke!' Shinji screams internally but keeps his mouth shut. Making his opponent angry wasn't a good idea. "Yamato -sensei, can you go a little easier next time? It feels like my arms are gonna break."

He doubts this will work, but he had to at least try. In response, Yamato smiled, not the usually nice and friendly smile, but a cold and sadistic smile. "I am already going easy on you. Not even using any jonin-level taijutsu style. Trust in yourself as I trust in your abilities, Shinji."

'Oy, oy, oy, that is overconfidence in me. I am just your everyday poor orphan that isn't that special.' Shinji complained in his mind but knew that saying anything from now on would be just a waste of energy. As Yamato got ready to attack, he tried to use the replacement jutsu, but when he brought his arms up, Shinji realized that they were still shaking. The sharp pain caused by the movement wouldn't allow him to make hand seals fast enough.

Fwish!

The sound of cutting wind was the only warning he got that told him Yamato is attacking. Shinji wrecked his brain, trying to figure out when he realized something. That front kick he did at first was something that many Taijutsu styles had, which made predicting the next attack impossible. Shinji didn't know the countless taijutsu styles that were, but something that Yamato had said before stood out in his mind.

'I am already going easy on you. Not even using any jonin-level taijutsu style.'

He repeated those words in his mind and Shinji knew one taijutsu style that also had a front kick in it and also knew all of the movements in it. He was taking a gamble here, but it wasn't like he had a choice. Closing his eyes, since they were only a useless distraction as he couldn't even see his opponent.

Using his hearing, the sound of cutting wind and grass being stepped on was the only thing he could rely on. He was betting everything on the taijutsu style Yamato was using being the Academy Basics.

As the sound of cutting wind got closer, Shinji's heartbeat seemed to increase. A split second before being hit, Shinji turned his head, using his forehead protector to block a hit to the head.

Baam!

Clang!

But this cost him, as the power behind the attack rattled his brain, and almost made him pass out. It was a punch to the side of the head, and Shinji had predicted it correctly, but he could feel his vision darkening and he was about to blackout.

'No!' he yelled in his mind, only his willpower kept him awake. But he could feel himself getting drowsier. He slipped to the ground, as his legs gave out.

"I don't think using your head was the best idea," Yamato instructed him as he casually started getting closer. "Using your legs would have been better, though that would have stopped you from running or walking for the rest of the battle. But using your arms would have been better, even though that would have put them out of commission for a time. Still, you would have been able to run away and last a little longer."

"Hehehe," Shinji chuckled, still feeling a little drowsy. "You're giving me too much credit. I didn't even have time to think clearly."

Yamato noticed him waving through some hand seals. "Good, you tried to distract me by talking. Also, when I say that you've done amazing, I mean it. But you should go to sleep now-"

Fwish! Fwish! Fwish!

Suddenly, three kunai shot towards Yamato, stopping the jonin from finishing his speech and approaching Shinji. Of course, he was able to easily dodge the attack. Looking towards where the projectiles came from, he saw a barely-standing Kato, clutching at his stomach, blood dripping down his lips. But he had a huge smile on his face. "C'mon teach, thought you were a jonin? I barely even felt that hit. Hahaha- *cough* *cough*"

Opposite of his grandiose words, Kato was injured heavily. Unlike Shinji, he hadn't been able to block the hit, and that showed.

"Kato, that was a good distraction, and I appreciate the way you want to protect your teammate. But any semi-competent ninja won't be tricked by that." Yamato remarked with a proud look on his face. "Don't worry, after taking care of Shinji, I will come and deal with you."

Just as he said, Yamato went towards Shinji, and this time he casually karate chopped him on the neck, knocking him out. But he felt something strange on the sensation.

Poof

'Shinji' was revealed to be a piece of log.

"How? There was no way I gave him enough time to go through all the hand seals," even Yamato was a little confused. But realization soon dawned on him. "Oh... he can use the Replacement Jutsu with less than the needed hand seals. With those wicked arms, he shouldn't have been able to go through more than two hand seals. That's not something a Genin should be able to do."

...

At the same time, Shinji was in one of the countless bushes in the forest. Leaning back, he made sure that his body wasn't visible to Yamato. Feeling the pain running through his body he winced.

'Fuck. I barely made it. Kota saved me there.'

As he glanced towards where Kota and Yamato were, he saw the jonin approaching his teammate. Now he was in a little bit of a dilemma, should he go and help?

Suddenly, Yamato started charging towards Kota and Shinji didn't have a lot of time to choose. Also, his teammate nodded, from the plan they made before the fight, this signaled that Kota was attempting to use himself as bait.

_____

[Pick one, and write your choice in the comments down below.]

A ○ Stay hidden and don't do anything to expose yourself.

B ○ Try to throw some projectiles. Though Shinji doesn't know how effective this will be with his injured arms. Also, this will likely expose your location.

C ○ Use the clone jutsu and transform the clones into something to distract Yamato. Then try to get Kota away from there.

D ○ Yell out and expose the hiding location. Shinji doesn't think this is smart. But it should help Kota... if he can move away from there.

_____

Status Updates:

[Crazily Ambitious] (New Trait!)

While you might not be the most talented shinobi out there. There is one thing that you have that trumps all others, and that's your ambition. You can put in hours of work towards your goal. Until you've reached your goal, your willpower will experience a boost. Shinji will now train whenever he can.

Replacement (E Rank) [Mastery 77% -> 80%] (2 hand signs)

_____

Relationships:

Kota 8/10 (He is inspired by Shinji to be something more.)

Sayuri 8/10 (She hopes Shinji archives his goals)

Chapter 6: Chapter 6 - Impostor Among Us 5

[C] Use the clone jutsu and transform the clones into something to distract Yamato. Then try to get Kota away from there.

——

...

Shinji knew that exposing his position was nothing short of defeat. So he tried to think of something, but no matter what, even wracking his brain wouldn't reveal a secret strategy to defeat Yamato.

Even though he was going easy on them, using only basic techniques and making himself deliberately easy to predict. Yamato's chakra, strength, speed, stamina, experience, and everything in between were leagues above him.

'After this fight is over. Whether I fail or pass, I must train harder.' Shinji had his ambition and wasn't satisfied with his strength at all.

He brought his hands up, his shaking was still there but the pain had subsided by now somewhat. Going through the hand signs, he created five clones and had them charge at Yamato as they came out of hiding.

"Ahahah! Yamato -sensei! I am here!" Yelled out one of the clones, drawing the jonin's attention for a split second. But that was enough for Shinji as he went out toward Kota, and his teammate was worse for wear.

"Hey... the plan was for you to attack him while I act as bait..." Kota muttered tiredly, not even having the power to speak anymore.

"It was a stupid plan," Shinji told him. "Also, do you want to get hit by him again?"

"No," Kota wholeheartedly refused. "Thanks for saving me. But if we fuck this up, I am totally gonna blame you."

"Yeah, yeah, now shut up and act like the damsel in distress you're supposed to be," Shinji picked his teammate up and put him over his shoulder like a sack of potatoes.

"Ow, your shoulder is digging into my stomach that was just kicked in," he complained. "Also I am not a damsel in distress, I saved your ass before."

"For a damsel in distress you speak too much," whispered Shinji under his breath, as an idea suddenly hit him.

He ran past the many trees, and a human-shaped silhouette came closer to him, and from the corner of his eye, he saw that it was Sayuri.

"Guys! Do you need help!" She yelled out in distress. "What happened to-"

Shinji didn't even let her finish and immediately threw a kunai at her. Sayuri's eyes widened in shock

The normal Genin Konuichi wouldn't have been able to intercept such an attack, especially at such a close range. Sayuri wasn't any different.

But a strange thing happened, as faster than either Shinji or Kota could see, her hand moved and caught the kunai mid-air. She smiled widely, something that seemed very unnerving on her usual face. "How did you notice?"

Poof

A cloud of smoke surrounded her, and as it cleared out, it's revealed to be Yamato. "You're sharp as well. You instantly caught on to what was happening."

"No," Shinji shook his head. "I was careless. Was Sayuri even here today?"

"Now that's some scary intuition you have there." Yamato's smile seemed to widen. "Technically, she was at the training ground, though she had been unconscious before she even met you. So yes, you're correct on your guess. The Sayuri you met initially wasn't her. But what gave it away?"

Shinji normally wouldn't explain something like this to an enemy as that would be dumb. But Yamato wasn't his enemy, and he needed to buy some time, for now, to let his arms rest a little and the pain subsides. "When you kicked Kota, you smashed him into a tree for maximum damage and so he wouldn't use the kick to make the distance between you two. You also attempted to do the same thing with me, it's probably an instinctual thing you do as a jonin to make sure you don't create too much distance between your opponent that would allow him to escape."

Shinji stopped there and didn't say anything anymore. Wanting the jonin to use his brains to try and figure it out, this way they would waste even more time.

"Oh, I see!" Yamato came to a realization, and his face lit up. "It was when I kicked Sayuri into the forest that you realized. And your guess is correct. I did that so when the clone that was transformed as her was destroyed, it would be out of your sight."

'Wait! Transforming your clones into something else. That is it! The answer I was looking for in this fight.'

Shinji had a realization, as soon as Yamato mentioned having his clones transformed into something else.

Suddenly he went through some hand signs and threw a shuriken, which multiplied into more illusionary clones of itself. Yamato just stood there and threw the kunai that he had caught before towards the real shuriken.

Clang!

"That looks impressive as if it is the shuriken shadow clone jutsu. But the hand seals are very different. Every ninja will be able to tell when you're using it if they see the hand seals you make for the usual clone jutsu." Yamato added, and he nodded in pride. "Though I don't think I've ever seen someone use the clone jutsu that way."

'Naruto seems like your jutsu might have some uses after all.' was what Shinji thought before he went through some more hand seals, creating clones of himself this time.

[Transformation: Sexy Jutsu, Harem Version]

POOOF

A large cloud of smoke surrounded the area around them, but it cleared up quickly and only naked women clad in skimpy outfits stood there.

Yamato was frozen in place like a glacier. Shinji's eyes sharpened like a hawk and he dropped Kota on the ground. "Kota! Now!"

"What the hell do you mean now?!" His teammate was confused as hell. "We never mentioned this in the plan!"

Shinji didn't elaborate anymore and took out some kunai and shuriken from his pouch, and threw them at Yamato without hesitation, and with the intent to kill. Anything less and he knew he wouldn't succeed in even scratching him.

Hearing the cutting air, Yamato's eyes widened, as if he came to his senses. One kunai grazed his cheek first, and the others all hit his body.

But Shinji wasn't fooled and immediately looked around, though nothing happened. Looking back, he saw Yamato's body drop to the ground, his eyes wide open in shock as a kunai had sunk into his forehead.

'Wait... don't tell me that he's dead!' Shinji panicked, immediately plans started forming in his head. He had to get away from Konoha, there was no way that killing one of their Jonin would be something they would let fly.

Who would even believe him if he said that the Jonin was distracted by female clones!

Suddenly, a hand grasped him by the back of his neck. "Good jutsu. Damn, I feel like only compliments are coming out of my mouth today."

Shinji felt cold sweat roll down his back, he had been caught off guard. Looking at Yamato's body, it slowly transformed into a wooden doll.

'Substitution? With a wooden doll?' Shinji knew that substitution was a jutsu that could be done with many things. But certain elements were more familiar to some. Like sand, mud, earth... the wood log was usually used by Konoha ninja as it was easier to replace with. But a wooden doll morphed to be like Yamato.

'There was only one person in Konoha known for using the Wood Style.'

Shinji's eyes narrowed at the doll, but he clenched his teeth and held in whatever he was about to say. Because deep down, it felt like he had realized something he wasn't supposed to. A village secret, the kind that people would kill to keep quiet.

"Oh~ that's a substitution jutsu without hand seals?!" Shinji exclaimed in mock shock. In his mind, he prayed to any God out there, that if they exist, help him out here before he gets himself to the T&I division.

"Yeah..." Yamato agreed awkwardly, giving the thing that he replaced with a side-glance. "I will help you with that later on."

"Okay, that's cool and all," the downed Kota intervened, laying down on the ground. "But can someone take me to a hospital? I feel like throwing up. Ate some nasty things today that mom cooked, I don't wanna taste that again as it comes out."

Yamato smiled and picked up Kota in a princess carry. "You should be a little more like Shinji. He took so many of my hits and looks as good as new."

"Yeah... No, my body hurts all over and the bones in my arms probably cracked," Shinji waved him off as they started casually walking outside of the forest. "By the way, did we pass?"

"Yes, you had already passed when you blocked my first attack, and when Kato used himself as bait, that only reassured my decision."

"Yep, MVP right here- *cough* *cough*" Kato tried to brag, but that instead earned him a coughing fit.

As they walked, Yamato had a smile on his face and they stumbled on a tied-up Sayuri, with Yamato's shadow clone waiting on the outskirts and reading a book. After a wave at the original, the clone dispelled itself.

...

While walking toward the hospital Shinji looked at his arms, the pain had somewhat subsided, but he couldn't help but contemplate how desperate things had been during the fight, and what he should have done better. He also understood that if he had been able to use Substitution Jutsu without the need of hand seals, none of the attacks would have connected and this fight would have at least been somewhat possible to escape if this had been a real enemy.

"Yamato -sensei, how long do you think it will take for me to catch up to you?" Shinji asked, and stared at his jonin teacher sincerely, showing that he didn't mean this in any disrespectful way.

Yamato thought for a little and shrugged. "I don't know, it depends on your hard work. Also, trust in yourself and your talent a little more, no other Genin would have been able to do what you did today."

"I doubt that," Shinji thought of Sasuke, and remembered how the Uchiha were known for their Fire Style Jutsu. "There were quite some talented guys this year, all those clan heirs too."

Suddenly, he felt Yamato's hand land on the top of his head as the jonin flung Kota over his shoulder like a sack of shi-... potatoes. He then ruffled Shinji's hair. "Hahaha, I have met many Uchiha in my days, and even fought a Sharingan wielder at one time. I don't know how fast you will catch up to me, but I feel like it might be sooner than most people think."

SIGH

Shinji sighed, unsatisfied with his progress at all. He had Tobirama's instructions in the book and had been training the Substitution Jutsu for days now, each day around 14 hours of training that jutsu. Yet, he hadn't mastered it. He felt his ambition burn brightly in his chest.

'I won't be able to master the higher-ranked jutsu if it takes this much to master just an E rank jutsu. A week... no, I will give myself two days to master the replacement jutsu, no matter what.'

His ambition wasn't just for show. Shinji didn't speak empty words when he decided to tell his teammates about surpassing Tobirama Senju.

...

Later on, Shinji was with an elderly doctor and he was running his palm around the genin's arms, head, and body. Yamato and his teammates were there too, even Kota had somehow magically gotten better and was able to stand up and walk around. The doctors called it; stupidity and hard-headedness. The jonin was also a little injured and had a scratch on his face. Before the replacement, one of Shinji's kunai had been able to scratch him.

Apparently, his excuse was that he had to see if his comrade in arms was okay. Yamato was still a little worried since he hadn't held back his power. But in the end decided to let Kota come along, better than having him move around without supervision or sneaking out.

"Heh! There is no way my comrade would be injured, we injured a jonin together. It's only a matter of time before I become Hokage, and he will be my right-hand man." Kota said while punching the air at an invisible enemy. When he suddenly winced and grabbed at his stomach. "Ow, ow, ow..."

The doctor checking on Shinji gave Kato a side glance and sighed. "Can you stop the idiot from straining himself?"

Sayuri crouched down, poking at Kato that was crawling on the ground while grasping at his stomach. "You okay? Also, I thought you wanted to just be an S Rank Ninja? Why Hokage all of a sudden?"

cough "Because that will help Shinji get all the jutsu that he needs... also a Kage has to be an S Rank ninja, right? " he muttered, surprisingly something insightful. "That's like killing two birds with one stone."

Even Sayuri was surprised. But then she chuckled. "Yeah, that's good and all, but Shinji seems more like the kind of guy to be Hokage."

"You're good," the doctor suddenly said, interrupting Kota from talking. "Though when you took that head injury, you should have passed out. But I have seen guys survive having screws in their skull, so this isn't that strange for a ninja."

Shinji nodded. "Then can I train today?"

"It should be okay, just don't do push-ups for today, just to be safe," the elderly doctor added.

Shinji was glad because today he had gotten some inspiration on how to do a seal-less Substitution. He planned to immediately start training the Substitution jutsu as soon as he got home.

"Anyway, now that you've all been checked to be okay, I have something I want to ask you, Shinji," Yamato suddenly said, his gaze showing the seriousness of the situation. "Since you told me your goal I have been thinking about how, as your sensei, I can help you achieve your goal. I had the doctor check about any allergies or something unexpected about your body. Thankfully, there seems to be nothing. But now, I plan to help build a perfect diet for each of you. We will start doing D Rank Missions from tomorrow. But we will also start training."

"So? What are you getting at, Yamato -sensei?"

"Shinji, what do you think I should help you train in the next two weeks?"

_____

[Chose one, and write the answer down in the comments]

A: Train Ninjutsu as Main, Taijutsu as secondary, and try to increase your body strength.

B: Just go all out Ninjutsu, and train nothing else. Learn everything that Yamato has to teach you.

C: Maybe try a hand in Genjutsu? Ask Yamato if it's possible.

D: Go all out in just Taijutsu and training physically.

E: Ask Yamato about what he should train.

F: Concentrate on Ninjutsu, Taijutsu, and training physically, equally. But try and study a little Genjutsu too during any second of free time. During the whole two weeks. (This option is only available due to Trait: Crazily Ambitious)

_____

Status Update:

Intelligence 3.2 -> 3.4

Ninjutsu 1.7 -> 1.8

Chakra 2.1 -> 2.2

_____

Relationships:

Yamato 7/10 (he full-heartedly believes in Shinji that...)

Kato 9/10 (though he complained, he was happy that Shinji came back for him)

_____

Chapter 7: Chapter 7 - Natural Talent? I can do it better. 1

[F] Concentrate on Ninjutsu, Taijutsu, and training physically, equally. But try and study a little Genjutsu too during any second of free time. During the whole two weeks. (This option is only available due to Trait: Crazily Ambitious)

...

Ambition molds a person's will to give it your all, towards a certain goal. A willpower drive so hard that makes one break and rebuild themselves stronger. Even though Shinji had trained yesterday after coming out of the hospital, and was now able to use the Replacement Jutsu with only one hand seal. He woke up like a lion, full of energy and ready to pounce into his training.

He remembered the answer he gave Yamato yesterday. He doesn't want to have a weakness, and a crazy idea has appeared in his head. Normally many people wouldn't be able to train all day long, but Shinji doesn't mind. What would he be doing if he wasn't training? Watching clouds? To him, that sounded boring as hell.

Walking out of his apartment after brushing his teeth, Shinji ran through the village and arrived at the training ground exactly at 6 AM. Yamato was already there though his teammates hadn't arrived yet. Excitement burst inside his heart, and it made his body shake.

"Well, you seem excited," Yamato smiled. "The meeting time was half an hour later though."

"Yes, I know, but I thought I could start earlier and do some warm-ups before everyone else arrived." Shinji smiled in excitement, he had never before had a jonin teach him. Jonin were top-class ninja, and each of them was a powerhouse in their own right. "So can we start training a little early?"

"Sure," the jonin shrugged and he started. "Have you ever heard of the tree walking exercise?"

Shinji frowned, trying to think where he had heard about it. Then he remembered that when he read the book the Hokage had given him, there were terms like tree and water walking mentioned. Though no explanations how to do them. "I have heard about it, but don't know how to do it."

"You don't?" Yamato looked a little surprised, almost bewildered, as if he had heard something outrageous. "Then how were you able to use Substitution with so little hand seals?"

Shinji shrugged. "I just kept doing it and tried to feel the chakra inside of me, regulating the flow. While at the same time trying to make it move the way it does when I do the hand signs."

His jonin teacher didn't say anything at first, having a contemplating look on his face. Walking towards a tree, Yamato put his foot on it and started walking sideways. "Can you do something like this?"

"No, I haven't tried it before," Shinji honestly said.

"Then this is the exercise we will do today. Before you start learning any jutsu, we need to get your Chakra Control to an acceptable level." Yamato instructed him, mentioning towards the sole of his feet. "To walk up walls like this, you just need to concentrate chakra into the sole of your feet. Keep a constant but concentrated flow. Do you know the leaf-sticking exercise? Where the teachers had you stick leaves to your forehead in the Academy?"

"Yes," Shinji nodded.

"It's kind of like that, except this time you'll try and stick yourself to a tree and walk upward," Yamato explained. "The longer you can keep that the better, if you can stay like that for an indefinite amount of time then that's when you can consider the technique mastered."

Shinji recounted everything that his teacher said and did the tiger hand seal to help himself concentrate his chakra easier and it worked as chakra gathered to the bottom of his feet. It was a little harder than normal to gather chakra there, but Shinji got the hang of it relatively quickly. He went towards one of the trees and put his foot on it, after tugging a little hit foot slipped, trying again he put a little more chakra, but this time the tree cracked a little.

The third time was the charm as he found the perfect amount of Chakra needed and he started walking up the tree, at first he kept his hand seal, but after a while, he let go and casually started strolling until he stood upside down in a branch.

"As expected," Yamato nodded, with a small smirk on his face. "You moved to the third step before doing the two before it."

"What's that supposed to mean?" Shinji raised a questioning brow. He didn't know what his jonin teacher seemed to be proud about.

"You can even talk while holding that position? You're either talented or just crazily hard-headed. I have never heard of someone trying to lessen the hand seal usage of a Jutsu without at first having basic chakra control," the jonin shook his head, but that confused Shinji a little. Because while Yamato's words were disapproving of such a method, the pride in his voice was unmistakable. "Now, before at least learning how to walk on water, don't try mastering how to do the Substitution without hand seals. It will just be a waste of effort on your part. Honestly, it's surprising you were able to go this far without even mastering the basics."

"So when do we start learning water walking?" inquired Shinji. Who was always hungry for progress. Feeling excited at the prospect of advancing, he could now feel that his hard work hadn't been for nothing.

"First try and keep walking around the tree for half an hour, and if you can do it without difficulty. It will show that you've mastered it."

"Can you give me a book about Genjutsu or something to read while I am doing this? Just walking around feels like a waste of time."

Yamato shrugged and took out a strange scroll, rolled out in the grass, and bit his finger to draw some blood. With a puff of smoke, a dozen or so books come out. He throws one of them at Shinji who catches it easily.

The jonin looked at Shinji, and couldn't help it as a smile made its way to his face as the genin started reading, while easily walking up and down the tree without seemingly any trouble at all. He didn't even seem to need to pay attention to holding himself up and was already doing so instinctually.

…

Half an hour later, Kota came to the training and he stumbled upon a strange sight, Shinji with one leg touching the tree, standing upside down, and reading a book. Normal people would ask why he is doing something this weird. But Kota was anything but normal, instead, he rushed at the tree, while yelling. "I can do that too!"

He was stopped from face-planting into the tree by Yamato grabbing him by the back of his shirt. "Oy, oy, don't rush in like a bird into a window. You've no idea how to even do that."

Kota smiled confidently. "Don't worry, teach. I can do it."

Yamato forced a smile, but his eyes were dull as if he was looking at a wall. No, even walls knew how to at least not to do something. Kota's IQ was in negative numbers here. "Stop, or I will smash your face into a tree before you can do it yourself."

The brash genin felt a chill run down his spine and rapidly nodded. "Y -Yes! Sir!"

..

Yamato explained to him what to do and Kota tried the tree walking exercise, but unlike Shinji, he had no success. As in, no progress at all. Yamato tests his Chakra by having him try and push as much chakra as he can against his hand, and as expected Kota had lower than average chakra reserves, which was normal amongst civilian-born children.

"It's weird if you're that bad at Chakra Control with so little chakra. Haven't you learned the leaf sticking exercise in the Academy?" The jonin was confused too, feeling that while Kota wasn't exactly inept in jutsu and genjutsu. He wasn't much better either. "You'll have to put more effort in taijutsu, especially if you want to become an S Rank Ninja. Ninjutsu will unlikely ever be your forte."

Sayuri had joined them too, and she had chakra reserves even lower than Kota, but she was good at controlling Chakra and almost did the exercise as fast as Shinji. The latter was standing in a tree, like a bat, upside down. "Don't worry too much about it, Kota. Something like this won't stop you right? If your fate is to be a normal ninja, then you simply have to change that fate."

Kota smiled, nodding at that and getting up resolutely. "Of course, there's no way that I am going to give up this soon."

Shinji had the ambition to fulfill and whether he liked it or not, didn't matter, but his genin team was bound to have a big impact on his journey as a ninja. For him to be worth anything, his team has to be amazing too. Though Kota didn't have the talent, at least he had the ambition. While Sayuri was the opposite, she was somewhat talented but didn't have the ambition to be more.

Yamato finally had prepared everything and called his students everyone over. "First, before you start learning any jutsu, you need to know your Elements. You can learn jutsu that belong to your element easier. Also, they generally cost less chakra to use. Though the opposite elemental jutsu to your natural element will be unlikely. For example, you usually won't see someone with a lightning element use wind jutsu. But that shouldn't be something you have to worry about, yet."

He shows them three papers the size of a human's palm. "Run chakra through them. We will see what elements you have," and Yamato displays by running chakras through his paper causing it to dampen and crumble to dust. "You see, since I have natural water and earth elements, I will have an easier time learning jutsu from them. But I would have a harder time learning fire style jutsu and lightning style."

Kota is the first one to step forward with an executed smile and grab the paper offered by his jonin teacher.

Shinji observed this by the sidelines. He knew that no matter what element he ended up with, then it should be okay. Initially, he had been a little nervous in case he would get water, since finding a teacher for it in the Land of Fire didn't sound easy. But since Yamato was a water-style user, then it shouldn't be a problem. Each element had its weaknesses and strengths.

Though he wished he had an element with a lot of destructive power and was easy to use. Something like fire affinity, which was the most common in the Land of Fire, is something he would be okay with.

"That's... amazing!" Yamato's exclamation brought him out of his thoughts and saw that Kato's paper had wrinkled, caught a little on fire, and some parts of it had crumbled into dirt. "Three natural elements, and with earth and fire counteracting each other means that the normal difficulty an earth-style user would have learning lightning jutsu wouldn't be there at all. But... it's a shame your chakra amount is so low. People like you with so many natural affinities are very rare, and even when they appear, they're usually Kekkei Genkai users."

Kota stared at the paper and frowned. "It feels like the heavens are playing with me. Using the carrot and stick method."

"Don't worry about it," Yamato reassured him. "Chakra can increase naturally with hard training and studying. Though I don't know if you'll ever be able to be a ninjutsu specialist. But ninjas mostly fight stealthily, so big explosions aren't that good."

"But they're so cool~" Kota whined, then he stared at Shinji. "But I guess we know who will be Ninjutsu Specialists. He'll be spamming jutsu in no time, and destroying armies."

Shinji within an instant was able to read Kato like an open book and see that his teammate was jealous. Or more correctly, he was envious of his chakra reserves. Both were civilians, but the distance of chakra reserves, something decided mostly at birth, destined the roads they would walk as ninjas.

At first, Shinji thought about saying some reassuring words to his teammate but understood that saying anything would just make him sound arrogant. Instead, he waited for Sayuri, who was staring at him. He caught her doing so and she just looked away, embarrassed.

'What was that about?' he wondered but decided to dismiss such thoughts. Sayuri went and took her paper, which quickly split in two.

"Oh? Wind. That's a little rare, but I know someone who can teach you about wind jutsu, so just channeling wind chakra through your weapons at least." Yamato nodded. "Also the same stands with you, Kota, I have a friend who's quite good with lightning. He owes me a couple of favors, though I can't promise on him being punctual."

Shinji takes this as his turn and drops down from the tree he had been hanging for the last hour or so. "Sensei, I don't think the tree walking exercise is useful to train my Chakra control."

"You and Sayuri should start water walking soon, but first, let's see what affinity you have," Yamato offered him the chakra paper and Shinji took it.

Looking at the small piece of paper he felt his heartbeat up to his ears, and the blood on his body seemed to freeze. This test would determine so many things for the future, and it wasn't something he would be able to change.

The paper in Shinji's hand split in two and became a little damp. Wind and water, he didn't know whether this was a good combination. This was a situation where Shinji wasn't too knowledgeable. He knew that Tobirama was well-known for his water style, but how good would he be with it? Yamato complimented his chakra amount, but just how good would that be?

Shinji had a vision of himself in the future, someone he wanted to be. While he was impressed by Tobirama, he didn't know exactly how much water-style jutsu added to his strength. After all, he didn't want to take the books he had in school as proof, since they were made with propaganda and a little brainwashing in mind.

"Two elements, wind and water, that's good since I can teach you quite a lot about water style. I would consider it as my strongest element amongst it and earth," Yamato seemed glad to be able to have the opportunity to teach Shinji something. After all, having another jonin teach his students wasn't something easy to do. "Anyway, we have to get you to learn water walking, and then you'll be able to start learning jutsu. Having good Chakra Control will help you master Jutsus easier."

Yamato, Shinji, and Sayuri walked away to learn water walking while Kato was left behind to keep trying to learn the tree-climbing exercise. The jonin then made some small talk and asked Shinji. "By the way, Shinji, what kind of Water Jutsu would you like to learn first? I have recommended C Ranks that would work well for you. It will help you get a handle on water-style jutsu. There's no wrong choice here, just which one do you think sounds better for you to start with?"

As the jonin explained to him about the basic jutsu he could learn. Shinji frowned, thinking about the answer.

———————————————

A - [Water Style: Wild Water Wave] (C Rank)

The user spews water from their mouth in a waterfall-like fashion to wash away the target. One can freely control the power of this technique by the amount of chakra kneaded and then released. While considered to be a basic Water Release technique, it has many variations.

B - [Water Style: Water Bullet] (C Rank)

The user then spits the water from their mouth as orb-shaped projectiles, whose destructive potential are determined by how much chakra is placed in them.

C - [Water Style: Water Prison] (C Rank)

This technique traps a target in a sphere of water; the water can either be drawn from the surroundings or expelled from the user's mouth. The water that the sphere is made from is noticeably heavy, which restricts the target's movements and can make breathing difficult.

———————————

Status Updates:

Replacement (E Rank) [Mastery 80% -> 94%]

Chakra Control 1 -> 2 (Average Genin lvl)

Genjutsu 0 -> 0.3 (Learning the basics of how it can be cast, dispel, etc)

_____

Relationships:

Kota 8/10 (he is a little jealous of Shinji and his chakra reserves)

_____

Chapter 8: Chapter 8 - Genin Days

A - [Water Style: Wild Water Wave] (C Rank)

The user spews water from their mouth in a waterfall-like fashion to wash away the target. One can freely control the power of this technique by the amount of chakra kneaded and then released. While considered to be a basic Water Release technique, it has many variations.

_____

Chapter 8 - Genin Days

...

"Water Style: Wild Water Wave sounds more versatile," Shinji explained his reasoning. "Also I can learn the other jutsu later, right?"

"Of course, now let me demonstrate," Yamato smiled.

They walked towards the pond and Shinji could feel the excitement rise in his heart. This was something he hadn't expected before. Sayuri stood by the sidelines and looked on as if expecting something.

Yamato went through the hand seals, which were just three of them. Which was a lower number than Shinji had expected, especially from a C Rank Jutsu. The jonin took a deep breath and gathered his chakra on his throat, lungs, and stomach.

<Water Style: Wild Water Wave>

BOoOOM!

Water exploded out like a miniature river and smashed into the pond, Shinji could feel the heaviness of the attacks as his dark hair floated about, and his brown eyes were filled with wonder. Yamato saw this and smirked. "So what do you think? Gather your chakra in your stomach, throat, and lungs. The hand signs will help you where to draw chakra."

Shinji nodded and went through the hand seals, and felt the chakra start to gather to certain points in the body, and he imbued chakra consciously along those points too.

[Water Style: Wild Water Wave]

Boom!

A small squirt of water came out at first, which was gentle enough to water plants. Yamato chuckled. "That's better than most," he said, trying to encourage his student. "At first most people can't even spew out anything. Especially with jutsu like these."

But Shinji wasn't satisfied with this, and put more Chakra into the technique, and the small sprinkle of water burst out like an explosive hose. Smashing into the pond, creating a big splash that covered Shinji in water.

"Good, amazing even," Yamato nodded with pride, his eyes shone while he glanced at Shinji. "You are having an easier time than most with this. Even I wasn't this good at first, and my water style is said to be one of the best in Konoha, for now."

Shinji nodded, understanding that jutsu aren't something that can be learned in just one day. Especially C Ranks, there was a reason such ocular Kekkei Genkai like the Sharingan were feared and revered. Because with one look they could 'steal' and 'copy' days of hard work effortlessly. Tobirama was also said to be able to pull out a lake of water in the middle of the desert, but he wasn't anywhere near close to that.

'I need to work harder.' Shinji's ambition burned even brighter and Yamato who saw this smiled and silently encouraged his student.

...

It didn't take long for Shinji's chakra to run out as a C Rank Justu took a lot of chakra and at most he could currently use it six to seven times. Yamato explained that this was due to Shinji not being used to the jutsu and wasting quite a lot of Chakra when using it.

But did running out of chakra stop Shinji from training? No, because he immediately started sparring in Taijutsu against his jonin teacher. Of course, it didn't take long for him to get pummeled to the ground by the jonin and quickly grow tired trying to keep up against an opponent many times better than him in everything.

In the end, Shinji was laying down on the ground, breathing heavily, with sweat making his clothes stick to the body. While his willpower hadn't perished at all, nor dimmed, it had gotten stronger. But his body couldn't keep up with his willpower and mind for now.

"Have you had enough yet?" inquired Yamato, glancing down at his tired student. "You should rest a little. Your chakra won't recover enough to practice ninjutsu until tomorrow. But your stamina will. Remember, you asked for this hard work."

Shinji nodded, but not long after, a frown appeared on his face. Yamato noticed this and thought. 'He is just a kid after all, and it's natural for him to get irritated at the amount of work. Does he finally plan to change his training schedule?'

But before Yamato could say anything, Shinji spoke first, expressing what he was annoyed at. "Sensei, I think having a Genjutu book to read while waiting for my stamina to recover would be even more efficient. Because this waiting would just be wasted time otherwise."

Once again, Yamato was surprised by his student's words and knew that he had underestimated Shinji's drive. But not long after, a smiling Yamato had a stack of books and created a water clone to hold the books while his students read them. Yes, Shinji was tired enough that he couldn't even lift his arms to hold the book.

...

By the end of the day, when Shinji's chakra regenerated enough, he would try, and cast simple genjutsu, like changing the color of his eyes. They weren't able to go on any D Rank missions during the first day, and Shinji slumped on his bed as soon as he came home.

But the next day, as soon as the sun shone on his face, he could feel the sun's heat radiation on his skin and immediately woke up. Waking up before even the alarm clock sounded out, Shinji was ready to go to the training ground. Today Yamato had said that they would have to complete a D Rank Mission before training because a certain someone (Shinji) would otherwise be too tired for a mission after training.

As Shinji got out of his apartment, he thought he heard something from the neighboring apartment, but decided to dismiss such thoughts and go to the meeting place early. This way he would be able to train the Substitution Jutsu until everyone else came too.

...

When he arrived at the training grounds, a smiling Yamato was there waiting for him. "Shinji, you weren't thinking of training, right? When I explicitly told you not to."

"Of course no," Shinji lied without missing a beat and he looked offended that his jonin sensei seemed to even assume that he would do something like that. "I am only here because my neighbor woke me up."

"Neighbor?" Yamato seemed confused at first, but then realization seemed to dawn on him. "Oh right, you should live close to him. Then I can understand that."

Him?

Shinji was confused, he had just made up the lie on the spur of the moment and even felt nervous that Yamato might not believe it.

'Who is my neighbor? Yamato -sensei seems to know him.' Thought Shinji, wondering why he had not met his neighbor until now. He had been living in the apartment for almost a week now, so not meeting your neighbor even once by now either meant that they were busy or just they never stumbled upon each other.

Shinji shook his head, dismissing such thoughts, and while he was surprised that his lie had somehow worked on an experienced jonin, he didn't want to lie to someone who would help him in his journey.

Especially about such a small thing, but at the same time, he couldn't just come out and say that he was lying.

The genin's thoughts clashed as he tried to think of something in a split second and the end he came with his answer. "Though sensei, if I had come here to train. Hypothetically, of course. Then I wouldn't have trained something that would drain my Chakra so much that it would leave me incapacitated to do the D Rank mission."

"What?" Yamato gaped, as realization drew on him. "Did you just lie to me?"

"Of course not, but I am just saying that if I had come here to train. I would have only trained the replacement jutsu which wouldn't waste a lot of Chakra." Shinji clarified with a cheeky smile.

The jonin got close and pinched his student's cheek. "How are you so good at lying?"

Shinji released himself from his jonin teacher's grip and his cheek had turned bright red. "I am not good at lying. You're just bad at noticing it. I made some stuff up."

Hearing that. Yamato's eyes narrowed. But Shinji acted casual, like anyone his age would. Due to his cautious nature, Shinji wasn't the kind of person who would trust someone easily. He had known his jonin teacher for only a few days. Yamato hadn't done anything untrustworthy, but Mizuki had been the same.

Still, he had enough common sense to not aggravate anyone and make it obvious that he wouldn't trust them with his life.

'Though with Yamato's power, I would be dead if he wanted to harm me. But as a ninja, it was good to be a little cautious.'

He noticed Yamato focused on him, thinking of something and then the jonin ruffled Shinji's hair, the smile on his face showing that he wasn't annoyed. "You'll make an amazing ninja," then the grip on the top of his head tightened, "Also you'll be a good liar. Oh wait, you're already good. You wanted to train Substitution, right? Then this is the best time to-"

Poof

Yamato's grip on him slipped, causing him to stop talking, and he saw that he was holding onto a log. It seemed like Shinji had already replaced himself. "Sensei, can you go easy on me?" a voice came from the forest. "I am a twelve-year-old kid, and hurting kids is abuse."

The jonin's smile turned frosty.

...

By the time Sayuri and Kota came, they had met each other on the road since they both were about to come here at the same time. But what greeted them wasn't the same training ground as yesterday.

Broken trees, the smell of ripped grass, some thick logs had been ripped from their roots. Water was everywhere, making the ground wet, and puddles were everywhere.

"What the hell happened here?" asked Kota, looking around curiously. He hadn't seen this level of destruction before.

"I don't know," Sayuri shrugged.

But her questions were about to be answered soon, as Shinji's body flew like a ragdoll. Their teammate's eyes were wide as an owl's and bloodshot as if he hadn't blinked in a while. All they saw next was a shadow shot towards Shinji and kicking his head off.

Both Kota and Sayuri's eyes widened in shock. Blood splattered out of the headless body, Shinji's decapitated head plopped on the ground. They couldn't believe what they're seeing. Shinji, dead?

"This time it's better!" suddenly the shadow that had killed their teammate started yelling out instructions. "While visually it was good, the smell of blood wasn't there. Any ninja with a brain would be able to tell that this is fake."

"Yamato!" Yelled out Kota recognizing his teacher's voice. He could feel his cautiousness slip into the wind. He pulled out a kunai, his grip tightening as he stared at his jonin teacher hatefully.

Poof

Suddenly, Shinji's 'corpse' transformed into a piece of wooden log. Leaving Kota feeling void... and kinda stupid now. So he just put the kunai back in his holster and coughed in his hand awkwardly. "I knew that of course. Shinji and I are eternal friends, we practically can communicate with just our minds. I was just trying to help trick Yamato -sensei."

Sayuri didn't say anything about his poor excuse, but her look said a thousand words. She obviously could see through such a poor excuse.

"Next time try and create a smell of blood, also during the kick, the log felt too light," Yamato's words brought the two out of their thoughts.

"What?!" Shinji's exasperated voice came from deep in the forest. "I have no idea how to do that? I don't even know any real genjutsu!"

Yamato suddenly stopped as he landed on the ground and with a thoughtful look on his face, he nodded. "Yea, you're right on that one. But still, I expect you to figure out such things quickly."

Shinji also came out of the woods, he was a little bruised, and his hair disheveled, and his eyes bloodshot, but seemed otherwise okay. "Damn, sensei, you should try and go slower. I can barely even see you," he rubbed his eyes, which he had to keep open for long periods. During the 'light' sparring, he didn't even dare blink, otherwise by the time he would open his eyes, Yamato's punch would be there to greet him. At least by now, he could do the Substitution without hand-seals. "Also weren't you the one who said I should try and keep myself in top condition when we start doing D Rank Missions?"

Fwish!

Suddenly, Yamato's body flashed again, and none of the genin could keep up. The next time his body became visible was when the jonin's elbow had sunk into Shinji's stomach. This caused him to spit out some saliva as his eyes rolled to the back of his head.

Poof

But again, Shinji had used Substitution, Yamato chuckled. "Am I that predictable?"

"Sometimes when you try to go easy on me, then yeah," Shinji was standing on one of the thick tree branches. "Though I have somewhat gotten used to your style. But I am not yet at a level where I can genuinely dodge even one of your real attacks."

Why was Shinji making himself visible and explaining his moves like a second-rate villain? So Yamato would be distracted and not notice the explosive tag behind the log he had used as a replacement.

pshhhht

Yamato caught on to what was happening, and his eyes widened.

BOOOOOOM!!!

The explosion was so loud that it made Shinji wince, and he tried to cover his ears. "That was expensive."

As the smoke cleared out, he felt his heart fall as a cocoon of earth greeted him, cracking up and revealing that Yamato was under it, a small nervous smile on his face. But he seemed to calm himself down easily. "Anyway, we should start doing the D Rank Missions."

Shinji breathed a sigh of relief at that, the only reason he hadn't been taken by surprise was due to his cautious nature. Which made him never drop his guard, even during a spar.

...

By the end of the day, Shinji had taken care of a baby as his D Rank Mission, trained himself to almost Chakra exhaustion, and as he walked home, it was almost evening, he looked towards the neighbors' doors. He wondered, should he try and get to meet them? See maybe if they were home.

Since Shinji remembered how Yamato reacted when he mentioned his neighbors, they might be some well-known ninjas. At least one of them was.

_____

[Pick one, and put your choice in the comment down below]

A - Check who your neighbors are.

B - No, just go to sleep. Who knows what Yamato might make you train. You need to be well-rested.

C - Check who your neighbors are. But even if they aren't there, wait for them to come back, at least wait a couple of hours. Shinji would like to know who he lives next to, and not be completely in the dark about his Ninja neighbors.

_____

Status Update:

Water Style: Wild Water Wave [Mastery 0% -> 31%]

Konoha Leaf Style (Basic) [Mastery 70% -> 91%]

Replacement (E Rank) [Mastery 94 -> 100%]

Taijutsu 1 -> 1.2

Genjutsu 0.3 -> 0.5

_____

Author Note:

In the Manga, the Substitution Jutsu was more detailed, and for example, when Kakashi was attacked by the Demon Brothers during the Wave Arc, his body was ripped apart, blood spilled, and his limbs plopped to the ground. The anime censored that detail, but I just wanted to show that what Shinji is doing is within canon norms. Not something he suddenly came up with.

Pics of Shinji are in discord if anyone is interested. You can join discord where I also post the dice rolls of the chapter and their effects. Since there are quite a lot of them and I don't wanna fill the chapter with dice roll numbers.

Discord:

https://discord.gg/wbwRTqd7jr

Chapter 9: Chapter 9 - Strange Neighbors

A - Check who your neighbors are.

_____

Chapter 9 - Strange Neighbors

...

The way Yamato spoke about the neighbor wasn't in a bad way and he wouldn't mind knowing another experienced ninja. Shinji knew that something could be learned from everyone, even the weakest ninja. But experienced Jonin usually had a lot to teach, even if they weren't his jonin teacher.

Shinji didn't have to wait, long, or at all really as he saw a man climbing up the stairs using only his hands while balancing a bag of groceries with his feet. At first, Shinji wondered if this was his neighbor, but he didn't have to contemplate for long as the green-wearing man stood in front of the door next to his apartment. This was where he had heard the sound coming from.

The man stood in front of the door, still keeping his eyes locked on the door, by the serious expression Shinji wondered what the man could be thinking about. Because while the man's green overalls were fashionably questionable, he still wore a jonin jacket. So he wasn't someone to be underestimated.

Shinji knew that with every jonin he had met until now, which hadn't been a lot, as it was mostly Yamato speaking of his other jonin friends. Still, from what he had gathered till now, no jonin was stupid. So while the man was looking at the door with a complex gaze, most people's first assumption would be that he was thinking about how to open the door since his hands were occupied.

But Shinji would never underestimate a jonin, so instead, he observed. Trying to understand what the man was going to do next. Suddenly, the green-wearing jonin turned towards Shinji and noticed him looking.

"Hey, there young man!" The jonin spoke loudly, due to the sudden yell, Shinji felt his heart skip a beat and unconsciously he had already prepared to use Substitution just in case. "Can you help me open this door?"

"Uhh… sure," Shinji felt his image of the jonin that had in his mind, smart, badass, stealthy, all of those impressions shattered like glass. Though he still learned something new today, jonin came with many… variations, and that his previous thinking had been flawed. "Though can't you just put the groceries down, and then open the door normally?"

The bowl-cut immediately frowned and Shinji's body clenched. Did he take that as an insult? Shinji hadn't meant to offend him, but the situation has become very nerve-wracking for him, he can't read the person in front of him. Maybe the green-wearing jonin was just this simple, but he didn't want to underestimate someone.

"Oh! That makes sense," Guy nodded, while still upside down.

Fwish!

He instantly changed position and before the groceries could even start falling as they were left in the empty air, the jonin caught them in his hands and took out a key. After opening the door, he had a friendly grin on his face, showing his white teeth that had a strange, unreal, genjutsu-like glitter in them. "Thanks, you man, what's your name by the way?"

"Shinji."

"Oh?" realization seemed to dawn in the jonin's eyes as a glittering light shone in them. "So you must be Yamato's genin?"

"Yes," Shinji nodded, seeing no reason to hide such a fact. "Do you know Yamato -sensei?"

"Of course, and I know about you too. Your sensei never stops bragging about you to whoever he can. Saying that not only are you talented but also very hard-working," the jonin nodded approvingly and suddenly his body started shaking, as the smile on his face grew wider. A flame seemed to burn ablaze in the jonin's eyes as he took a deep breath and yelled out. "That's so YOUTHFUL!!!"

Shinji got chills down his spine when he heard the last word. But he tried to keep a nonchalant look on his face. While the jonin's actions seemed ridiculous, Shinji still noticed how fast he was. Going from a hand-stand position to sitting up faster than not only he could see, but before the groceries started falling was an amazing feat.

'That speed is something that even Yamato -sensei would fall short on. I can at least feel the wind move when Yamato -sensei attacks. But with this guy, I doubt I can dodge even knowing where the attack was coming from.'

Of course, Shinji knew that his examination of a jonin-level person would be lacking. But he still saw clearly that this silly-looking man, with caterpillar-like eyebrows, was nothing short of a beast in a human's body. "By the way, what's your name?" Shinji couldn't help but ask. "Since we are neighbors after all."

The man's glistering teeth seemed to shine brighter, and he gave a thumbs up. "I am Might Guy! Konoha's Green Beast!"

Shinji nodded in respect, needing his head, about to go back to his apartment and rest after a long day of training. But suddenly, he heard footsteps climbing up the stairs, and this time it was an old man

He had gray hair, which was tied in a short ponytail, and the old man was carrying a big cooking pot on his back? He looked like a kind grandpa, and he smiled at Shinji. "Hi there new neighbor, I see that you've already met Guy."

Shinji hadn't met his neighbors at all during his stay here that was now almost a week, yet was able to meet two of his neighbors in one day. They might have been on a mission, so that was likely why, but Shinji knew that it was common sense to not ask a ninja, especially a jonin, what missions they were on. He considered himself lucky, and couldn't help but feel safer with having a jonin like Guy as a neighbor.

"Oh, Maruboshi," Guy greeted the old man respectfully and smiled. "Our new neighbor, Shinji, is quite youthful."

"Hahaha," the old man laughed happily. "You call even an old man like me youthful, Guy."

After some small talk, everyone went to their apartment and during that conversation, Shinji learned that the old man was a genin too. That was a little surprising, since by that age a genin is either dead, which is the more likely possibility, or they should have enough money saved up to retire. Even the enthusiastic ninja usually only work in administrative positions by that age.

Still, Shinji didn't bother thinking too much about that, as after washing himself he slumped onto his bed and the sweet darkness of sleep consumed him. As an aftereffect of training hard, and pushing himself to the brink of Chakra Exhaustion daily, he could fall asleep easily.

…

Two weeks passed within the blink of an eye, and for Shinji, those two weeks were a blur of Ninjutsu, Taijutsu, and Genjutsu. Oh yeah, sparring with Yamato too. Each day his muscles were broken, and his body bruised, but his will never faltered.

He kept going strong, training 16 hours a day. Even when eating, or shitting, he was reading a Genjutsu book or something. So essentially he had trained for 224 hours in two weeks. Even if someone trained a whole month, they would have to train over seven hours daily, and that was still a lot.

Essentially, Shinji had compressed months of training within two weeks. He had to go sometimes to the hospital for the medic-nin there to have a look at his condition. But with a perfect diet, and consistent, robotic-like training.

...He had achieved something remarkable.

Shinji stood in the training ground where he and his team usually met. As usual, everyone was here. By now Kota had gotten the handle on water walking, which was considered good progress for the average ninja. Especially since he trained hard too. But in comparison to Shinji, he was lazy.

Sayuri looked on with a strange look in her eyes, smiling at Shinji. There was something in her eyes that he couldn't quite put his finger on. But dismissed the thought as there are more important things right now.

Yamato stood opposite of Shinji and warned the other two genin. "Stand back," after saying that he looked at his student. As a teacher, he couldn't hide the look of pride in his eyes. He might have pulled a couple of strings to have Guy give him a detailed scroll on the Strong Fist that had his notes on. Yamato didn't hold back and did everything he could to have Shinji grow fast. "How is your progress on learning the Strong Fist?"

"Kind of slow," Shinji muttered, his eyes sharp like a hawk. While his body was ready to jump at any moment.

"I will try and get Guy to help you personally in the future. Though no promises there as he has his own Genin Team." Yamato nodded and suddenly started waving through hand seals.

Shinji immediately started waving through hand seals too, but he only needed to do one while Yamato did three.

<Water Style: Wild Water Wave>

[Water Style: Wild Water Wave]

Both took a deep breath, mirroring each other. The water that spewed out of their mouths created a wave that would engulf the other and it was like a miniature tsunami.

BOOOM!!!

The waves crashed, splattering all over. Sayuri and Kota who were quite far away already jumped back, not wanting to get hit by the harsh water drops as they were like rocks due to the massive pressure created with the clash.

"This doesn't look like a fight between a genin and jonin at all," remarked Kota, amazed as Shinji dashed, walking on the water as if it was second nature by now. His speed was nothing to joke about either as before the water droplets could touch the ground he was in front of Yamato. Unlike two weeks ago where he could barely defend, now he could attack too.

Yamato still had a smile on his face, clearly showing that to him Shinji's speed wasn't at a level where it could yet be dangerous. But as he looked at Shinji's eyes, the jonin's eyes widened. The world around him shifted, turning into a desolate place, a destroyed Konoha, multiple heads of Konoha jonin's heads were on pikes. The blood felt so real, he could smell it.

The Hokage was in a crucifix, suddenly a pale man with snake-like eyes came out of the darkness. But Yamato did the tiger hand seal and yelled out. "Kai!"

The world around him shattered like glass, though he could still smell the blood. He saw that Shinji's knee was about to hit his chin, but the difference in speed was apparent as within a split second Yamato caught the genin's knee and his fingers sank into it.

Poof

But that was revealed to be just a log, surrounded with sizzling paper bombs.

Shinji, the real him, stood atop one of the trees, he had never thought that a D Rank Genjutsu would be able to stop Yamao for more than an instant.

BOOOOOM!!!

The explosion surrounded Yamato and created a crater, which had the water from the previous water jutsu fill it and create a small pond. Shinji smiled seeing this, but his eyes widened as the air behind him twisted, and he was able to duck below a fast kick aiming for his head.

Taking out two kunai, Shinji pounced like a tiger at Yamato, and without hesitation stabbed the pointy metallic weapons into his jonin -sensei's body. By now the Shinji from two weeks ago would have panicked at the thought of maybe killing a jonin but by now he knew better.

POOOF!

A large cloud of smoke surrounded him. "Shadow Clone," he muttered, looking around but his sight was interrupted. But Shinji felt a heavy feeling in his stomach, as the sound of rushing water entered his ears. He contemplated using Substitution, but the jutsu wasn't made to be used in long distances, and by the sound, the Jutsu was a wide area one.

<Water Style: Giant Vortex Jutsu>

[Water Style: Water Wall]

So he was forced to use the only B Rank jutsu he knew, putting as much chakra as he could into the jutsu while throwing a kunai upward.

BOOOOM!!!

As his water wall clashed with Yamato's jutsu, his water wall was destroyed, but it still protected him long enough for the smoke to clear up and Shinji to regain his vision. Not a second later, the water hit Shinji harshly, making him spit blood.

But that Shinji turned into a kunai, showing that he had used Substitution, the one that he had thrown upward, due to the split-second lag after using Substitution, which wasn't instantaneous, Shinji had been forced to waste a huge chunk of his chakra. The real Shinji was mid-air. Not a position he would consider favorable, since he couldn't move well up there. Though it wasn't like he had a choice, to begin with.

"Shit," he swore, annoyed. Sensing the next attack was barely done as the air seemed to shift, but Shinji knew that no matter what he did now, he wouldn't be able to dodge it. A giant torrent of water slammed onto him, he winced in pain, as he could hear his ribs crack. "Fuck, can't you go a little easier?"

While inside the water, Shinji was being slammed towards the ground, but he had to stop that from happening or he would be out of the fight by then, too injured to continue anymore. But to his surprise, he felt a shift around him and he saw Yamato's figure who was inside his own jutsu and he smiled at Shinji. This made the latter have a look on his face as if he swallowed a peeled lemon.

"I am not using earth-style jutsu, that's good enough of a handicap for you," Yamato explained himself.

'Yeah, and you also are not using that other thing. But of course, I can't say it out loud.' Shinji thought. He started waving through hand seals, ready to use a genjutsu that would give him an advantage.

But Yamato wasn't going to let that happen, as he kicked Shinji's wrist and the power behind the kick was enough to dislocate the wrist. What surprised the jonin was that he didn't scream in pain or anything, his eye only twitches a little, that was the only sign that he was in pain and he threw a punch towards Yamato's face.

Of course, the punch was easily blocked by Yamato's palm, but Shinji smiled as he used the jonin's hand to complete the hand seal. This surprised Yamato, and that surprise was enough for Shinji to take advantage

[Paralysis Jutsu]

Yamato's body froze for a split second, but he broke out of it quickly, just as Shinji was about to slam into the ground. Yamato noticed the slight weight shift in the water and knew that Shinji had used Substitution.

BAAAM!!!

The water pressure cracked the ground like a spider web, and Shinji was nowhere to be seen. But the genin appeared from the trees, Yamato narrows his eyes in suspicion, a little unsure if that was the real Shinji or just a water clone. The jonin also could feel his chakra running a little low, having used multiple A-Rank Jutsu.

He assumed that Shinji must be low in chakra, but the genin could will-power through most injuries and pains. So it wouldn't be weird for the jonin teacher if somehow his student forced himself to enter Chakra Exhaustion. Shinji was smart enough to not do something detrimental like that, but Yamato knew his student's competitive spirit.

While Shinji's Chakra Reserves weren't quite to Yamato's level, the latter had used a lot more chakra than his student. This was mostly due to Shinji's mastery of the Substitution Jutsu, which cost very little chakra and could be used to dodge jutsu that would cost a lot.

sigh "What an annoying brat to fight," Yamato complained loud enough, to make sure Shinji heard him.

The Shinji that had made himself appear smiled. "I am sure that if you went all out, then you would be able to defeat me easily. I'm just a simple genin after all. Using earth style you would have been able to go underground and take me by surprise quite a lot."

Suddenly Yamato looked down and saw that the water he was standing on felt thicker, heavier, and immediately he attempted to jump away. Five figures resembling Shinji came out of the water.

[Water Clone Jutsu]

Each clone extended their hands out, having gone through multiple hand seals already.

[Water style: Water Prison]

A dome of water formed around Yamato, and a heaviness settled around him, locking the jonin's body shut. It felt more like being encased in heavy wet concrete than water. But Yamato slowly turned into a wooden doll, with his form.

Shinji winced. Feeling the chakra exhaustion settle in, he didn't want to be incapacitated for weeks. So he let exhaustion take effect as he stumbled back and started falling.

Fwish!

Within an instant, Yamato appeared behind him. "This is the second time you make me show something that I am not supposed to," the jonin glanced towards the wooden doll. "Though I have a sneaking suspicion that you already know that."

"Hehehe," Shinji chuckled, feeling tired, both mentally and physically. "I don't know what you're talking about Yamato -sensei. I forget a thousand things a day, and will make sure this will be one of them."

Yamato sighed, but a chuckle escaped him. "Well, this will be the last spar we will have in a while. These spars between us won't go unnoticed for long. You need to rest.``

"But-"

"No," the jonin's gaze turned harsh. As he laid his student on the ground softly. "Remember Shinji, you still have a life. At your age, you should be out there experiencing life, making mistakes, sometimes looking like a fool. That is a different experience that will give you certain understandings that a ninja needs to know. Growth isn't something you can rush, or it will be stunted."

Shinji stared at Yamato with a dull look in his eyes. "Before you interrupted me, I was going to agree. I am not stupid to overwork myself too much. During this time I was injured almost every single day during training, and that sucks. I am not masochistic."

"Oh… so you understand," Yamato said awkwardly.

"Obviously," Shinji replied. "I know that if I try to work too much I will become a burned-out 'genius'. Someone who can only follow a road already paved for him and not make his own, like that most people can reach jonin-level at best," his eyes narrowed and overwhelming hunger and ambition shone through them. "I want to surpass Tobirama Senju, and he was one of the ninjas known to have created more jutsu than even his brother. Though I also know that training must be done in moderation."

The jonin nodded proudly. "That's right. By the way, what do you think about our team going on a C Rank Mission? I want to hear your opinion on this too. Normally genin don't' get C Rank Missions so early, but you're an exception."

Shinji could see that Yamato -sensei wasn't worried if he was ready. The one he seemed more concerned with was his teammates. Who were having… average progress, that grossly paled in comparison to Shinji's. He contemplated what to say next.

_____

[Pick one, and put your choice in a comment down below]

A - "Yes, we are ready. I will make up for Kota and Sayuri's shortcomings. That's what teammates are for, after all."

B - "No. We aren't ready yet. They need to train for a little longer and find something they're good at before going on a C Rank Mission."

C - "Yes, but only us two need to go on the mission and leave Sayuri and Kota behind." Shinji feels like this choice would ruin the team dynamics.

D - "No. I don't want my teammates to see how apparent the difference in power between us has become. It might make them feel bad."

E - "No. Let's continue with more training. For now, we need to become stronger. Maybe I could get Guy to help me with training Taijutsu while you concentrate all your efforts on helping them. We need to all be ready for this, not just me."

Chapter 10: Chapter 10: Poison Flowers and Tragic Thorns

E - "No. Let's continue with more training. For now, we need to become stronger. Maybe I could get Guy to help me with training Taijutsu while you concentrate all your efforts on helping them. We need to all be ready for this, not just me."

_____

(A/N: In discord, there was a vote and a part of this chapter we will see things from Sayuri's perspective and how she sees things.)

….

Chapter 10: Poison Flowers and Tragic Thorns

…..

-Sayuri POV-

"No, let's continue with more training," Shinji muttered to Yamato.

"What do you think they're saying?" Asked Kota, seeing that they were saying something. But he was unable to hear them due to the distance.

"I don't know," I lied to him without missing a beat. Kota was unlucky to be in the same team as someone like Shinji, the latter had already outshined him so much. Surprisingly, he isn't too envious. This would ruin most teams.

Shinji smiled at our jonin -sensei. "For now, we need to become stronger. Maybe I could get Guy to help me with training Taijutsu while you concentrate all your efforts on helping them. We need to all be ready for this, not just me."

Damn it, couldn't he be a little more selfish here? Shinji, you need to get used to killing soon. No, he probably knew that by now. He was always perceptive as hell. But someone like him had his reasons.

Looking at the wet lush grass below my feet, I couldn't help but wonder how long I would have to continue and play this role. Someone like Kota, and maybe even Yamato could be fooled, the latter most likely wouldn't suspect someone as young as me. But Shinji was the problem here, he was like a hawk. Always on guard, and growing stronger each day.

Though Yamato was suspicious too. The files Konoha has on him are nonexistent before he became a jonin teacher. So he either was an Anbu, or something much... much darker.

I was supposed to fail the Genin Exam. Then I would have joined the Genin Corps and gone MIA, missing in action and been presumed dead. That should have been it, Shinji and Kota weren't supposed to be anything special. Just some deadbeat average ninja.

I could have had better grades in the academy, at least above the banshee, Sakura, but that would have put me in the same team as Naruto, the Nine-Tailed Jinchuuriki. That's a ticking time bomb I didn't want to anywhere close to. Maybe then I would have orchestrated that team to fail, though Sasuke was an Uchiha and Kakashi had the Sharingan too. So the elders might have him pass anyway, and the team put together anyway. In the end, I must be average not only to not stand out but also because I was scared as hell of the Nine-Tails, who knows just how well that seal might go and when it will go off.

Yamato helped Shinji get back up to his feet and they both walked towards us. I glanced towards the young orphan that had suddenly revealed that he was talented as hell. But my heart stopped for a second, as I saw him staring right back at me.

Has he noticed something? I swallowed hard, and smiled, trying to sink into the background. C'mon, I'm just the ambitionless girl on the team. Don't suddenly start paying attention to me when even the jonin here doesn't. If I had known this, then after Shikamaru, Shinji would have been another teammate I would never want to have. They're too damn smart for their own good.

"Eventually, we will have to take a C Rank mission. Kota, Sayuri, I will be pushing both of you as hard as I can," Yamato -sensei's words brought me out of my thoughts. Reminding me where I was and that Shinji wasn't the one I should be considering the biggest threat with the jonin standing right next to him. "Anyway, Sayuri, can you help Shinji get to the hospital? You can come back later. Just have the doctors check that everything is okay."

Jeez, he is such a worrywart for Shinji. If he was going to be worried like this, then shouldn't have left him to train like a mad man for two weeks straight. Shinji has something wrong in his head too, what people have that kind of crazy willpower at our age?

Orochimaru must be kept in the dark about that. I don't know why he wanted me to keep an eye on Sasuke Uchiha, but getting Shinji involved in something like this...

He...

This wasn't logical at all. But, I don't want to give him up to Orochimaru. I knew how the snake man is. Giving Shinji to him was the same as killing and torturing Shinji with my own hands.

"Sayuri, let's go," Shinji said with a smile on his face. Mentioning me to follow him. Like always, he was very energetic for someone about to enter Chakra Exhaustion. "By the way, do you want some sweets?"

Like always, his voice played at my heartstrings. This was so unfair. Why did it have to be this guy? It's a stupid reason why I don't report him. All started with a lunch box during the graduation day. Saying that he had made lunch for all his teammates when the box barely had food for him, yet he shared it.

I am protecting someone just because they gave me some badly cooked food. Now that I think about it, doing that makes me like some kind of dog. Loyal to someone just because of some bad food. I have had leftovers that tasted better, but...No, it wasn't about the food. It was much more than that.

Such thoughts went through my head in a split second and I smiled. "Yes~ I will buy you some udon."

Making sure to hold my breath a little to make my cheeks flush red, and act embarrassed. I played the perfect act of a girl who had a crush on a boy. Whether he saw this or not, I don't know. Is this even an act anymore? I don't know that either.

"Right, you should buy me some since I have wasted a lot of money buying explosive tags," he said. Yeah, he wasn't that romantic. What kind of guy makes the girls buy them lunch?

"Yes," I answered before even thinking it through that well. "But we have to make sure that you're well physically."

Acting all worried and nice to him. Was it an act? I don't know anymore. Ever since I could remember I have been acting and lying. It's become a little confusing to even tell lately.

We walked amongst the streets of Konoha, Shinji acting casual, but I could instinctively tell that he had his guard up. It was always like this. The people ignored us, only kids sometimes taking notice of our headbands and smiling. They probably had dreams of becoming a ninja.

...

When we arrived at the hospital, Shinji had a plastic bag full of snacks. Most of which were bought with my money. I could smell the medicine as soon as we entered. A lot of shady stuff happened in this place due to a certain someone. Did the Hokage know about that? Probably not, but Danzo probably did. That guy was as sketchy as they can be. He's even worse than Orochimaru on that part because the old war-hawk can influence Konoha internally.

Many talented kids in the orphanage disappear, of course, the matron says that they moved away. For the Will of Fire things he spews and how he considers everyone in Konoha as family, Hiruzen is like an absentee father. Not knowing when his 'children' even go missing, But no one pays attention to orphans, that's why it was easy to join them.

We arrive towards the office of the doctor Shinji usually does his check-up with, he is an old man, one of the best doctors in Konoha. As always, Yamato -sensei had gone far and beyond for Shinji. He is a good jonin teacher, I know for sure otters wouldn't have done even a quarter of this.

Shinji kept looking at the door, but stopped before entering and suddenly turned around to look at me.

I blushed, playing the part of the embarrassed girl, and asked. "A -Aren't you going in?"

He shrugged and smiled at me, the gentle look on his face didn't shift and he gave me a thumbs up and handed me the snacks bag. "I don't know what's worrying you. But here, you can have these as a gift."

After that, he entered the doctor's office and I was left stumped. Okay, so he was even more perceptive than I thought.

As soon as he closed the door behind him, the blush on my face turned back to normal. Looking down at the snack bag, I couldn't help but sigh. "What do you mean by gift?" I muttered under my breath. "I was the one who bought most of these."

I should go back to Yamato now, as he had only told me to escort Shinji here. But I will have to pull the act of a pathetic girl in love because I must make sure his medical file doesn't fall in the wrong hands.

Suddenly, I sensed a hand on my shoulders and instinctively almost pulled out a kunai and stabbed the hand. But I remembered that we were in a hospital.

"Sayuri? What are you doing here?"

Immediately, a cold chill ran down my spine. I felt my knees buckle like noodles as fear gripped my heart. Trying to keep composure was useless as I felt his fingers harshly clenched into my shoulder. "Calm down, don't look so suspicious."

His nonchalant voice didn't help at all. Turning my head around, I saw Kabuto, with a harmless smile on his face. "Why're you here at the hospital? The time for your report hasn't come yet."

"Sh -Shinji is having an examination," I told him the bare minimum, trying to defuse the situation. That was when I noticed that there were no other people in the hallway. Shinji! Are they planning to do something to him? Looking towards the door, I wondered if I could break Kabuto's grip and go-

"Whatever you're planning, I wouldn't do it," he remarked in a joking voice.

What should I do now? Think! I need to think of something!

My heart felt like it was going to burst out of my chest. No, I needed to calm down. Would they dare do something like kill or kidnap Shinji in bright daylight? That would be too dangerous.

"Anyway," Kabuto released my shoulder. "Since you're here anyway, how about you give the report now?" that wasn't a request, and we both knew that. "Since you're stuck with that team anyway, is someone in it that would interest Orochimaru -sama?"

"No," I answered immediately, having regained my composure. "Kota isn't anything special and Shinji is barely above average," I lied to him with a straight face. "At best they can become some Chunin."

"Hmmm~" Kabuto hummed, seeming to think about something. "You wouldn't lie to Orochimaru -sama, would you?"

"Of course not, I value my life and wouldn't want to die a painful death," I answered without missing a beat. "It would be a stupid thing, to die for someone who has only been my teammate for not even a full month."

Kabuto nodded. "Keep in mind, that no matter how they act. If they know what you are, then those same 'comrades' will not hesitate to kill you. As long as you spy for Orochimaru -sama, you'll at least have his protection. But if you lie, no one will be there to help you."

Yeah, I knew that too. Shinji would probably slit my throat if he knew who I was working with. It's only a matter of time before he figures it out, and it's the same with Orochimaru, he will figure it out too when he figures it out that I have been lying for Shinji.

I guess my lifeline is until the Chunin Exams. After that, I'll probably die.

After saying what he had to, Kabuto walked away, leaving me contemplating my despairing life. So this was it? I have until the Chunin Exams, where Shinji will undoubtedly stand out. Suddenly the doctor's door opened, and the person I have done this all for came out.

Would he cry when I die? Will he hesitate when he slits my throat?

The best I can hope for is that he doesn't notice what I am until the time of my death comes. At least that way, he would regard me with fond memories in his mind. I was going to die anyway, so better do so without regrets and help pave the road for someone like Shinji.

****

Shinji glanced at Sayuri and noticed that she seemed even more worried now than before he went into the doctor's office. He didn't know what was bothering her. He could think of one thing that might, and it was how much faster he was progressing than her. "You shouldn't worry, I am sure after you find something you're very good at, you'll grow stronger. I was the same in the academy before I had access to a jonin teacher and better jutsu."

Sayuri came out of her stupor and glanced at Shinji, smiling, like always when she looked at him, she had a small blush on her cheeks. "That's not what I am worried about."

"Hm?" Shinji was perplexed and instead looked at the snacks in her hand. "You didn't eat any of them?" he wondered if maybe she didn't like sweets. "Anyway, don't be so down. After I get some money, I will buy you something that you like."

Suddenly, a small smile came to her face and she chuckled. "Shinji, if something were to happen to me, would you be sad?"

"Obviously yes," Shinji answered. He had delayed taking the C Rank mission because he was worried his teammates weren't ready yet. Also, he wanted the team to get used to working with each other and as a real team. "I would be really sad if something were to happen to you."

Sayuri looked down, her hair casting a shadow in her expression. Hiding her face from Shinji's sight, but he could still see a strange smile on his face, and when she looked back up, she had a bright look. "Then I guess, I should work harder too. I don't want to get hurt on a mission, because you would be sad."

"That shouldn't be the main reason why you would be worried about being hurt," he whispered under his breath. But decided to not get to say anything, because as an orphan himself, he knew that not a lot of people cared about them, or if they were hurt.

..

As they walked through the hospital hallways, they had some small talk and Shinji noticed that Sayuri seemed happier than usual, but he couldn't figure out why.

"Anyway, I gotta go training, see you later," as soon as they were out of the hospital, she ran off.

Shinji waved at her, and looked around, seeing the streets of Konoha. For the first time in a while, he had a free day. He had nothing planned for the rest of the day, and he didn't have enough Chakra to train ninjutsu.

_____

[Pick one, and put your choice in a comment down below]

A - Stroll around Konoha, and look around. Enjoy yourself and try some foods that you might like. Maybe you could meet some fellow ninja or interesting people.

B - Try and find Guy. See if you can get him to teach you Taijutsu. The faster you start this, the better.

C - Go to the Hokage Mountains and appreciate the view from up there.

D - Look through some ninja weapon shops and try to find a weapon that you would like.

E - All of the above, at the end of having fun, you try to find Guy.

Chapter 11: Chapter 11 - Local Adventure

E - All of the above. Don't concentrate on just one, you could have fun and keep an eye out for Guy too if you see him. (New Trait: Multitasker)

_____

Chapter 11 - Local Adventure

...

Shinji thought about what to do today, and he had all day to himself. He decided to stroll through his village, trying to memorize the markets and ninja shops, which were quite abundant in a ninja village. Still, this sense of having nothing to do felt weird, not necessarily bad, just weird.

But he dismissed such thoughts for now and went towards a dango shop, getting three sticks of dango and enjoying the sweets in the shop as the warm sun heat gently touched his skin. With a smile on his face, he enjoyed the sweets and as he was about to get up he saw someone looking at him. They wore a Konoha headband as a bandana, with a dark mask covering their face.

Shinji took back his empty plate of dango towards the counter, something that normally would be done by the waiters. But he decided to do this as a sign of politeness. An old man stood at the counter and looked at him weirdly. "Can I help you with something young man?"

Shinji only smiled politely, handing him the plate and some money. "Keep the change. But I have a question. Don't look too intently, but that man, the one with the mask and Konoha headband, is he a regular?"

The old man's eyes sharpened, and he smiled, knowing how to play along. Shaking his head, he whispered. "Do you need to call for help?"

Contemplating what to do next, Shinji shook his head slightly. "No, this is just something I was curious about. As he might be one of my teammates under transformation jutsu. But don't tell him."

Hearing that it wasn't anything serious, the old man breathed a sigh of relief. The adults in Konoha knew the rules regarding any potential suspicious individuals or spies. But Shinji knew that if anything happened, and the village got involved right now it would be just he said guesswork. For all he knew, this man might have been here coincidentally or had been sent by the Hokage. But in this case, he assumed the worst, as his cautious nature wouldn't allow him to be careless here.

Still, Shinji acted casual, putting his hands in his pockets and acting nonchalant, as if he hadn't noticed anything, and walked out. Situations like this, if handled carelessly could blow out of proportion.

He went around and tried some more food stalls, and stayed in the public eye and places that ninjas frequented. This way his tracker, which was still keeping an eye on him, couldn't do anything and this gave Shinji enough time to come up with a plan.

...

In the end, Shinji decided to go atop the Hokage Mountain, with the strange man following. To most people, this might seem like an empty place, but Shinji remembered from a certain book in the Academy which described how the civilians would escape to the shelters in this mountain in case of a disaster. If there was one sure place that ninjas would stand guard, it would be this mountain, the gate, and the Hokage tower. The latter two were too obvious and his plan would be figured out.

Though he couldn't sense anything, Shinji knew that some Anbu were likely already observing him. After all, the village wouldn't want any spies to sabotage the place where the shelters were. Though he didn't have concrete proof of this, it was a logical thing that anyone would do.

Shinji stood atop the mountain, the Hokage heads carved on the mountain he was standing on. Looking down, he could see people moving about their day, from up here they were small as ants, every now and then he would catch a glimpse of ninjas jumping atop roofs.

"If you had noticed me, then say something, bastard," the person who had been following had an annoyed look on his face and got closer. He was taller than Shinji by quite a bit, showing their differing ages.

"Why are you following me?" asked Shinji, turning towards the man, a calm gaze in his eyes. Though he was a little low on chakra, he had prepared everything, and taking care of this man wasn't the end goal.

'Someone sent him, he doesn't seem like the kind of guy who is a leader of anything. Even his competence to follow orders is questionable. Someone has an interest in me, and I don't know who. Maybe this guy could help me figure it out after some... persuading.'

"Heh, the chunin exam is coming soon. So I decided to scout my competition a little."

'That is a lie. He doesn't seem like the kind of person to do that, and his hand twitched as if he wanted to grab a kunai. Also, the look in his eyes isn't of someone afraid of competition. This guy was likely very confident in his abilities.'

"I see," Shinji acted as if he believed him. "Then what're you going to do now that you've been found out?"

"Well," he smirked, taking out a kunai. "I will have to figure out how strong you are by myself!"

Shinji wasn't surprised by the turn of events. But he also realized something else, someone wanted to know how strong he was. Even if he wanted to show others what he got, due to the low chakra he wouldn't be able to.

Taking out a kunai of his own, Shinji waited for his opponent to come close, and as soon as he did, he slashed at him. Liquid sorted out of the attacker, but it wasn't blood, but water. Shinji's eyes widened in surprise as he felt someone behind him, slither around his limbs like a snake, grabbing onto the. The man's arms and legs had become soft, almost rubber-like. "H -How? Who are you?!"

"Heh, I guess you aren't anything special after all," the man chuckled, clenching his hold on Shinji tighter, making the younger man wince. "I am Misumi Tsurugi, and have your life in the palm of my hand brat."

"W -Why are you doing this?" Shinji's breath became haggard as the man tightened his grip.

"Trust me brat, you don't wanna know."

"Is that so?" Shinji's voice came from behind Misumi, and the latter gaped as something in his shoulder.

Poof

The 'Shinji' he had been strangling showed that he had been a log all along. Misumi glanced at his shoulder and saw a kunai had dug deep into it. He attempted to turn around and grasp his opponent.

Crack!

A loud, bone-breaking sound rang out, as the hand he had extended to grasp into Shinji was broken like a twig. A small piece of bone had punctured the skin and made itself visible to the outside.

"Ahhhhh!!" Misumi yelled out in pain, grasping into his arm, falling to his knees.

"You seemed quite sadistic when you thought you were strangling me," Shinji remarked, crouching to his opponent's point of view. Misumi saw this and played his screams to a higher level, waiting for a chance to attack. "Anyway, tell me who sent you."

"I -I..." Misumi tried to act pitifully, and as soon as he saw Shinji get closer, he used his un-broken hand to try and grasp into his opponent, but he was surprised when his hand slipped right through and his opponent's figure flickered and dimmed into the air.

A sharp pain sprung into Misumi's extended hand. "AHHHHHH!!!"

"That was a clone," stated Shinji, who was revealed to be standing to the side and had thrown a kunai. "No one is stupid enough to get close to an enemy whose abilities are suited to strangle someone. Or maybe your rubber-like body was made that way so it could fit into closed spaces?"

Though Misumi didn't say anything. The nervous, and fearful look on his face was a clear enough answer for Shinji. But now he had to choose what to do with this guy. He kept in mind that there were likely some ninjas observing him.

Still, Shinji knew that since he was within the village boundaries he couldn't act recklessly and kill a fellow Konoha ninja in broad daylight. So with that in mind.

_____

[Pick one, and put your choice in a comment down below]

A - Torture, light torture. Mostly genjutsu, and try to make him talk. After that, call out to the ninja nearby, if there are any. If no one answers, then take Misumi as a prisoner and try to find a Chunin or higher ranked Ninja and report what happened.

B - Go hard on the torture. Use Genjutsu and physical. You need to know who is after you and what is happening. After that, you will call out to the ninja, and if there aren't any, find some to hand over your downed opponent.

C - No torture. Just call out the ninja, if there are any around. If there aren't then go and find them, with your downed opponent in tow.

D - Just walk off. You don't want to get involved in this any more than you already have. Shinji thinks this might have Misumi grow to become someone who will be a thorn to his side.

E - Just torture him for information, and leave him there for any ninja to find. If they don't then, that's all there is to it.

_____

NOTICE: In your answers write if you want to cripple Misumi:

Example:

None at all, you have done enough. You don't want to possibly destroy his Ninja career.

A little (break his legs),

Medium (break all limbs and fingers),

High (shatter as many bones as possible, just try to keep him alive, there is a chance of death), he won't ever be a problem anymore, Shinji will make sure of that.

Chapter 12: Chapter 12 - Ruthless

A - Torture, light torture. Mostly Genjutsu, and try to make him talk. After that, call out to the ninja nearby, if there are any. If no one answers, then take Misumi as a prisoner and try to find a Chunin or higher ranked Ninja and report what happened.

-How hard is Shinji going to try and cripple him? Medium. (New Trait!)

_____

Chapter 12 - Ruthless

...

Shinji looked at Misumi, a downed opponent that was quite sadistic in his methods. He knew that if the positions were switched, he would be having a very painful experience. So with that in mind, Shinji's eyes turned cold. "You just picked the wrong opponent."

Fear glimmered in Misumi's eyes, as he struggled to get up, could see in Shinji's gaze that what was going to follow wouldn't be pretty. "W -Wait man, I wasn't going to kill you!"

Knowing that he wasn't good, nor did he have any experience in physical torture, Shinji decided against it. But for now, he knew that Misumi was a dangerous guy and wouldn't hesitate to strangle him if it came down to it. Doesn't matter what orders his superior gave him, once it came down to it, he would kill Shinji to survive if needed.

So understanding that Shinji walked closer and pulled out a kunai."Don't worry, I don't plan on killing you either," after saying that, he stomped Misumi's legs, though his bones could dislocate themselves and gave him the ability to make his body soft. He was still human, and his bones could be broken in this banner. "Sorry, but you're a dangerous guy and I am just a newly graduated Genin. Can't take the risk of you going after me."

By now, Shinji was speaking out loud not for the guy he had defected. But the Anbu, or any ninja hiding around here. Shinji could feel his downed opponent's bone break as his foot pushed down to the ground with all the power he could muster. It wasn't a nice feeling and the scream of pain that followed almost made him wince. But Shinji held strong, his decision set in stone. As he looked at the wriggling enemy, he imagines himself, and the tortures he might have had to suffer if the position were switched.

"AAHHHH!!!" Misumi screamed out, drooling as his lower face mask fell off. Shinji noticed that he was quite average-looking, just another face in the background. They were similar in that.

Crack!

Bones were broken, fingers shattered, Shinji was merciless and even used his mask to gag his victim. He asked one question after another, but Misumi never said anything more than scream out in pain. He wasn't doing this to torture him, and while the pain of bones breaking might be painful, this was so he wouldn't become a problem any time soon. Shinji made sure that the man who had attacked him wouldn't be able to wave hand seals for at least a year.

'This much damage should take about half a year to heal, and by then he should be able to use his arms which would make him dangerous again. By then though, I should be in a league where he can't even touch me anymore.'

Ever since becoming a Ninja, Shinji never was illusioned with the goals of grandiose without the need to get his hands dirty. His will wasn't weak to falter at this sight either. By the end of it, Misumi's limbs were twisted strangely and his fingers in both hands were broken. Though Shinji hadn't seen anyone do one-handed seals, he didn't want to take the risk here.

Taking the gag out of his opponent's mouth, Shinji coldly asked him. "Are you ready to talk? Who sent you after me?"

"H -hey, no, no one sent me after you, *hic*" tears rolled down his face as he cried. This made Shinji doubt what he was doing for a split second. But he remembered how the fight had gone.

"What about the time you had me in a chokehold and didn't let go at all?" Shinji inquired. "The strength you were using would have almost broken my neck if I hadn't used substitution earlier. Now, I don't care about your excuses. Tell me what I want to know. Who sent you?"

[Demonic Illusion: Hell Viewing Technique]

Shinji put Misumi under genjutsu that would show his worst fears but as a D Rank Jutsu. It didn't have any effect, and he just clenched his teeth even though he couldn't break out of the genjutsu.

Sighing, Shinji glanced towards the trees, where if any ninja was here that's where they would likely hide. "Hey, you saw it right? He attacked first. Also, him being this resilient just proves that he has something to hide."

No response came from the trees, he sighed again, unhappy that he had to carry Misumi down the mountain. 'Well, this can be considered as training at least. So that should be good.'

But as he turns around, he sees a ninja silver-haired ninja, with an eye patch covering one of his eyes and a mask covering the lower part of his face. "Yes," agreed the ninja, glancing at the downed genin and crouched down to look Misumi in the eyes. "This guy is hiding something. That resistance against pain isn't normal. Though you should learn how to inflict pain better, the tips of the finger are the best point to start. Under the nails are a lot of nerves."

Shinji nodded, but internally he was surprised, not having sensed anything when the man moved. "I will keep that in mind. By the way, can I know who you are?"

"Kakashi Hatake," the jonin answered casually. "Also, weak genjutsu of D Rank is unlikely to work during torture either. When people are tortured they can say anything to get out of it, so you have to be careful about that too," Kakashi picked up the downed person by the hair and pulled up his headband, revealing a scar over his eye, and the eye was red with three tomoe slowly swirling. "You need hypnotic genjutsu if you want to get information."

<Sharingan: Genjutsu>

Misumi seemed to come to his senses for a split second as his eyes cleared up. He looked at Kakashi with hate. "I am-"

"Shut up, unlike him," he pointed at Shinji. "I can put you through a world of pain just for fun. So who do you work for?"

Misumi's body shook as his eyes became dull, his pupils enlarging. "Orochimaru."

Even Kakashi was surprised by the name. "Why were you following Shinji?"

"I-" the man was about to speak, but Kakashi's red eyes spun and he immediately put his hand in Misumi's mouth and pulled out a tooth.

"No dying on me either," Kakashi whispered. "I don't know what countermeasures your master put in place so you don't spill information. But things won't go his way."

Shinji looked on in wonder, this was a pro at his work. Kakashi seemed to know what his victim was going to do before they even did it. But that sense of wonder didn't last long as the name mentioned before rang in his mind. He remembered a certain history book he had read in the academy. Orochimaru, Jiraiya, Tsunade Senju, the Three-Way Deadlock, and the Sannin. They were three of the strongest ninja Konoha had produced in the last half of a century.

"Uhhh…" Shinji uncomfortably intervened. "Sir Jonin, am I involved in this now?"

Shinji did NOT want one of the strongest ninjas out there having an eye on him. Or possibly being angry at him.

"Oh yeah, you're super involved," Kakashi said nonchalantly. "Also you'll have to help me with the paperwork in this. Because I was just enjoying the view until you came. Do you know how busy I already am?"

'Not busy enough apparently, if you have time to relax atop the Hokage mountain and enjoy the view.'

Shinji kept his thoughts to himself. He didn't want to anger a jonin, and while Kakashi's demeanor seemed casual, he saw how the jonin handled Misumi. As a genin, Shinji didn't want to be on the receiving end of that.

"I have students too, and am already two hours late."

Two hours? Then why are you here enjoying the view acting so unconcerned about it? Shinji had many questions but decided to keep them all to himself.

Kakashi suddenly frowned and went through countless hand seals in a split second, at speeds he hadn't seen before. He couldn't even tell what hand signs were being made.

<Sealing Jutsu: Corpse Freezing>

"Seems like our friend here has a neuron poison at the root of his brain. We have to take care of that before continuing the questioning." Kakashi waved his hand and three shadows came from the trees, surrounding the download body. They were all Anbu, and Shinji swallowed his fear, he hadn't known any of them were there. If they were enemies...

Fwish!

They disappeared as soon as they came, taking Misumi's unconscious body with them. Each of their movements was done without mistake and they were in sync.

"Anyway, wanna go get some ramen?" Asked Kakashi, with an eye-smile.

"Didn't you say that you have some students?"

"Meh," he shrugged. "It's only two hours late. We have plenty of time. In around half an hour all the information your attacker had in his mind will be spilled. Another half an hour to take care of any other spy in the village that we might discover. After that, I will be right on time."

The way Kakashi explained it, he seemed to think this was 'right on time'. Shinji only looked at the jonin dully, glad he didn't have someone like him as a teacher.

But as he thought about it, a chill went down Shinji's spine. Do they suspect him too? Or maybe this is just the village being cautious. Maybe that was why Kakashi was so insistent on having him along.

"Still up for some ramen?"

_____

[Pick one, and put your choice in a comment down below]

A - "Sure."

B - "No. I am busy." Shinji feels like this option could make him seem suspicious.

C - "Sure. But can you help me find a jonin named Guy?"

D - "Sure. But can you help me find a good weapon's shop?"

_____

Status Update:

[Merciless] (New Trait!)

Shinji won't have mercy against his enemies and won't hesitate when fighting them. He is willing to cripple someone if it comes down to it.

_____

Relationships:

Kakashi 6/10 (Decisive, smart. Knows a lot more than he lets on. Future T&I or Anbu?)

———

Chapter 13: Chapter 13 - It's All About Drive

C - "Sure. But can you help me find a jonin named Guy?"

——————

Chapter 13 - It's All About Drive

...

Shinji thought about what to say, he contemplated not saying anything at first and just agreeing and going along with Kakashi. But if he needed to also find Guy, especially now that it seemed like a very strong Ninja was after him.

Since Guy was a jonin, and Shinji didn't know when he might go on a mission and not be seen for weeks or more. But Kakashi, as a fellow jonin, had more access to information like that. So at worst, he wouldn't waste time looking for him.

"Sure. But can you help me find a jonin named Guy?" Shinji requested, feeling a little nervous asking a jonin such a favor. "Since I was planning to find him after some sightseeing."

"Hmmm… okay, but after the meal." Kakashi agreed without much of a problem. "Though you'll have to answer a couple of my questions for that favor."

He was glad the silver-haired jonin accepted. It had taken him almost a week to meet Guy, even though they were neighbors, maybe they had different schedules? Shinji shook his head, dismissing such thoughts, and walked next to Kakashi, as they walked down the Hokage Mountain. Of course the ninja way, but sticking to the side of the wall.

Shinji felt a little awkward, not knowing what Kakashi was like at all, and the man himself seemed to be very nonchalant about things. "By the way, Yamato speaks a lot of good things about you."

"He does?" Shinji wondered, feeling strange, but a smile came to his face. 'Yamato -sensei is the best. Now at least most jonin should not have a bad first impression.'

"Yeah, kinda a lot. To the point that it's annoying." Kakashi clarified, his one exposed eye glancing at Shinji and then at the feet he was controlling Chakra. "I can see why though. It hasn't been long since you have graduated and your Chakra is very stable. Also, your Chakra network is very expanded. I only know one other Genin your age that has more Chakra."

Shinji tried to think of who had more Chakra than him in his age group, and the only two people who came to mind, Naruto and Sasuke. He wasn't a sensor, but Naruto probably had more Chakra since the prankster wasn't able to even experience Chakra Exhaustion even when the teachers tried to have the students experience and how it feels to have little chakra and get used to it.

Though Naruto later missed the second and third lessons in later years, in the first year Shinji remembered how monstrous the yellow-haired Uzumaki's chakra was. '

'It really is a shame that he never really tried that hard and in later years became a prankster instead of learning jutsu and paying attention in class. Behind Sasuke, Naruto was the one with the most potential in the class, though he never seemed to show that potential.'

"Naruto? Right?" Shinji guessed. "There is another one too, Sasuke has more Chakra than me."

"Not any longer," Kakashi said, his calm eye staring at Shinji. "You must have gone through some hellish training. But your full Chakra should be a little more than Sasuke's by now. Even Chunin will have a hard time matching your chakra unless they are specialized in Ninjutsu."

Shinji was a little shocked by this news, he had never thought he would surpass someone like Sasuke. Well, if it came to a fight, it might be different as Chakra amount doesn't decide a battle between ninja.

But still, seeing that his training and hard work hadn't been for nothing made a sense of joy burst in his heart.

Kakashi only observed Shinji by the corner of his eye, and once he saw the huge smile that unconsciously appeared in the genin's face, the jonin couldn't help but mutter. "Seems like Naruto and Sasuke will have quite a problem in the Chunin Exams."

"Huh? Did you say something?" Asked Shinji, not having heard what Kakashi whispered about. His excitement had gotten the better of him for that split second, but he was back to being calm.

Though he wouldn't admit it out loud, those two weeks of training had been a little taxing on his mind. But right now, he felt like he could just go back and train all over again. Now, he can't wait to start that kind of training again. Shinji took a deep breath, trying to calm himself down and thought about things with a calm mind.

'No, I can't do that right now as the situation with the spy is a little complicated. Also, this isn't just about working hard but working smarter too. Having Guy's help would get rid of some bottlenecks that would waste time in Taijutsu.'

He wanted to go and train so bad, becoming strong like this was the thing that brought him joy. But his will somehow prevailed through all this. Still, his mouth slipped. "Do you mind if I train while eating?"

Kakashi looked at him weirdly, as if he was seeing someone unpleasant when looking at Shinji. "You remind me of someone. I can see now why you would want to look for Guy."

They arrived at the end up the mountain, and Shinji immediately used Chakra to stick to the ground as he walked to count as training as it would take more effort to walk this way. Kakashi glanced even more weirdly when he saw that, it seemed like he didn't want to be here. "Can't you just have a normal reaction? Just be arrogant that you have more Chakra than an Uchiha."

"What's there to be arrogant about?" Shinji asked, his eyes focused on his hands, training to go through hand seals faster. "I simply trained harder. There's nothing to be arrogant about. As soon as I stop training he will easily surpass me. Only a fool would act like that."

...

Once at the ramen shop, it was a nice place that had a nice smell to it that made someone hungry just by entering. Kakashi sat down like a normal customer. Shinji on the other hand was doing squats while training to go through hand seals.

Ayame, the ramen shop owner's daughter, is a slender girl with long, dark brown hair, large black eyes, and fair skin. She wore a white robe with the sleeves folded, a sort of dark blue apron with ribbon ties at the top, and a bright white bandanna. "Is he okay?" she pointed at Shinji.

Kakashi waved his hand. "Don't mind him, kinda my fault he became this way. I wish I had said no, I don't wanna be here when Guy comes."

Ayame, already used to seeing weird ninja, just shrugged. "Okay, the usual Kakashi?"

"Yeah."

"What about you?" she asked Shinji, and the young genin looked at her with passion in his gaze. Any other girl might have misunderstood this. "Also don't look at me like that. It sends the wrong message to a girl."

"Oh, sorry," Shinji came out of his stupor. "Also get me a bowl of miso ramen, thank you."

He went back to training. Sometimes working hard wasn't just about doing so for a week or two, but about consistency. Shinji was also worried about Orochimaru and what the man wanted, and all of that combined with his ambition had made him want to train harder and smarter. While these times of training might seem something that wouldn't help, if he works hard every day, then it will add up into something that others won't be able to surpass.

"By the way, your chakra network is okay, right? And you don't have a desire to suddenly start wearing green spandex?" Inquired Kakashi suspiciously.

"What? Of course not," Shinji looked at him weirdly. He could understand that green would help one as good camouflage in a forest or grass field. But why would it have to be spandex? "If I need a certain color for camouflage I can just use the transformation jutsu and change just the color of my clothes."

"...That's a good idea actually," Kakashi admitted. "So you're like a smarter and genuinely talented version of him."

"Of who?" Shinji wondered.

"You'll know soon enough."

Ayame smiled. "Your name is Shinji, right? How old are you?"

"I am twelve years old," Shinji answered politely, but clearly wasn't paying too much attention or even looking at the girl.

"Oh, that's a shame," she sighed dejectedly. "So, what type of girls do you like?"

"Never really thought about it," Shinji answered without missing a beat. Ayame was about to continue talking, but she noticed Kakashi giggling weirdly while writing something in a notebook. This caused the young girl to blush in embarrassment and walk away, acting as if she was going to help her father in the kitchen.

Kakashi only kept chuckling in amusement. While Shinji was only concentrated on his hand seals. For showing him such an amusing scene, the Copy Ninja decided to help the young genin a little. "When you go through hand seals it needs to be instinctual. Some ninja just need to think of a jutsu and their hands go through the signs without having to consciously try."

Shinji nodded, thankful, and tried to do the hand seals with his eyes closed.

...

After eating some ramen, and an embarrassed Ayame not showing herself anymore. Kakashi and Shinji walked outside of the shop. Though there was one thing Shinji was curious about, how will Kakashi find Guy?

That question of his was answered as soon as Kakashi took a deep breath and yelled out. "Guy!! Let's have a challenge!!"

Shinji looked at him weirdly while at the same time practicing hand seals. The yell wasn't even that loud and Konoha was a big village. But he was proved wrong as suddenly a green flash landed on the ground in front of them as if sent by heaven.

Booom!!

"It is I, Konoha's Green Beast, ready to accept the challenge of my eternal rival."

'Shouldn't Guy also have a genin team? Why are these jonin who are supposed to be busy have so much free time?'

"I can feel someone overflowing with YOUTH!!" Guy peered at Shinji like a hawk and made him a little uncomfortable. But Shinji didn't interrupt his training, hand seals, and doing squats, even as Guy smiled at him with his sparkling white teeth.

Poof

Kakashi burst into a puff of smoke, making Shinji wonder how long he had been a clone. But that thought went to the side as he bowed towards Guy at a perfect 90-degree angle. "Guy -sensei, I know you have a genin team, but can you help me-"

"But of course! How could I refuse someone with such OVERFLOWING YOUTH!!" Guy agreed without a second thought. Shinji felt weird, he had been a little worried if Guy would accept to teach him, but his worries were for nothing.

"So when do we start training?"

"Right now! Let's run with our hands and try to go and find Kakashi! Let our youth burn brightly!!"

"Do we know where he is going? Do we have a way to track him?"

"Use your YOUTH to sense him!"

"..."

...

Evening came about, Shinji lay atop one of the roofs, breathing heavily, but he had a smile on his face. "What a weird day."

After Guy gave him some instructions he went to find Kakashi, as Shinji had been too tired to follow. He also gave him a schedule where they would train together, and since they were neighbors, it would be easy to find each other. Guy was mostly going to point out any mistakes he made, as he couldn't train him all day, due to having his own Genin Team.

Also, the spy he had caught had quite a lot of information in his mind. He wasn't informed exactly what happened. But both Guy and Kakashi had to get involved and shinobi were running around like flies as if looking for something... or someone. So it had to be something big. During that time, Shinji made sure to stand atop the roof, in clear sight of the ninja running around. Just in case anyone got the idea to kidnap him. He didn't know the situation in deep detail, but decided to be cautious, and play it safe.

While contemplating, Shinji couldn't help but think about another thing he had realized when training Taijutsu. Unlike some basic Taijutsu Styles, the Strong Fist was harder to master than most out there, but it was also one of the best styles of Taijutsu Shinji had ever seen. He was glad to have asked Guy for help, otherwise, it would have taken ages to learn.

Remembering just how much of a monster Guy was physical, Shinji couldn't help but wince. Stamina, strength, speed, even amongst Jonin he seemed too fast.

That was when he remembered that he had one last thing to do today. "Right, try and see if there is any suitable option for a weapon out there."

Looking around, he saw some ninja weapons shops and went to the closest one. As soon as he entered, he saw that there were many weapons on display. With bright lights all around, making the weapons on display easy to look at.

The smell of metal resided in the air, and Shinji theorized that these same weapons must be made close by. Maybe to the back of the shop? But since it was nighttime, they wouldn't be using the anvils as it would make too much noise.

"Hello there," the shopkeeper greeted. He is a bald burly man with a friendly look on his face. "What can I get ya?"

"I don't know yet, just came to get a look at what weapons you have. I don't have the money to buy a weapon made of Chakra Metal yet, but maybe buying a weapon with normal steel first would help me get used to it." Shinji remarked, as his eyes wandered towards the many weapons.

———————————

[Pick one and put your choice in a comment down below. What Shinji thinks about the weapons will also be put in the choices too.]

A - No weapon, only kunai, and shuriken when needed. Buy some more of those and some explosive tags. Maybe might decide again later on if he wants to learn how to handle a weapon. But for now, Shinji feels like he is too busy with everything else.

B - Kusarigama, blade on a chain. Has become somewhat of a famous weapon type after being used by Hanzo the Salamander. It's good for close and mid-range. A very versatile weapon, but Shinji thinks it's a little exotic for a weapon so finding someone to teach him might be hard. Still, it was worth a thought.

C - Brass Knuckles shaped like a trench knife. Short-range and good in a close fight, works well with Taijutsu. Maybe they can be thrown for long range? You still had kunai for throning, so these would normally be used in just close range.

D - Tanto. A short sword that is used usually by Anbu. Easy to hide, and finding someone to teach him was just as easy.

E - Chokuto Sword, a straight katana. A good weapon in close range and well balanced. Shinji wondered what kinds of sword styles Konoha had? He hadn't studied them a lot.

F - Spear. Do Ninjas use spears a lot? Shinji doesn't know exactly but hasn't seen anyone use it. Maybe a good weapon for a civilian, as even someone unskilled can use it with relative efficiency. What about a Ninja?

G - Staff. A good blunt weapon, versatile in its usages, but not as lethal as a sword and needs good strength to do critical damage to a ninja.

H - Nunchaku. A weapon with two metal rods attached by a chain. Hard to use masterfully, and doesn't seem to have the versatility of a metal staff.

I - Learn how to use many weapons. Shinji thinks this would be a little inefficient when training.

J - Long Sword. Samurai?

K - One-handed short-range axes. Bandit? Why are those weapons here? Do bandits come and buy them from Konoha? Or maybe just a display case.

_____

Author Note: Shinji was supposed to annoy some people, luckily he didn't. If you want a more detailed explanation of things, and want to see the dice rolls which are used to calculate luck, join Discord:

https://discord.gg/wbwRTqd7jr

P.S: Amongst the choices, E, Chokuto Sword is the same type of weapon Sasuke had during Shippuden. Just in case the explanation wasn't clear enough. Also the new trait is due to Shinji doing something that would normally annoy people, but luckily it doesn't. So with that is how he got the trait.

P.P.S: If you like the story. Give it some love by sending some power stones. I love writing it and I hop you love reading it.

Chapter 14: Chapter 14 - It's All About Power 3

E - Chokuto Sword, a straight katana. A good weapon in close range and well balanced. Shinji wondered what kinds of sword styles Konoha had? He hadn't studied them a lot. (literally won by 1 vote more than 2nd place)

———————

Chapter 14 - It's All About Power

…

Shinji looked through the many weapons, from the most exotic like the weapon that Hanzo used, to others. But in the end, his eyes settled on weapons that he could master and at last learn how to use from someone. He saw the tanto, a short sword, good for someone his age, but not overall good usage once he grew stronger.

"How much is this?" he asked, picking a chokuto sword. A straight katana, the balance was perfect and swinging it down, it left an arc of steel in the air. This would also give him more range, something he needed against adult ninja. "Easy to use too."

"4000 Ryo," answered the burly shopkeeper, looking on with a melancholic smile. "Be careful not to die out there."

"Of course," Shinji smiled back at the man, taking out his wallet and paying for the sword. "Also better keep a chakra metal sword in store for me."

'There goes half my budget. I need to get a C Rank soon and get some money. That way I could get myself a Chakra Blade sooner.'

"Heh, of course, I will, brat," muttered the old man, covering his eyes with his big hands, while using the other to wave him away. "Now make sure you don't die or I will haunt you down to the afterlife."

"Family, and losing someone dear to you," Shinji muttered quietly as he walked out of the shop, looking at the new sword that he had just bought. Showing it, the sword's edge glimmered in the moonlight. "Family…" that word sounded unfamiliar to say in his mouth. Never having it being applied to him.

As he walks back home at a slow pace, Shinji thinks of many things, but he also wonders if maybe someone was following him. His senses didn't pick up anyone, nor were there any signs of someone following him he could pick up. He didn't have something like a sixth sense of feeling it when someone looked at him. But it was just a simple deduction.

After all, he had been involved in a spy discovering mission. Leaving him alone wasn't a good idea. Shinji wondered if calling out to them would be weird, they wouldn't harm him since they were here to protect… probably. Still, Shinji was on the more cautious side and was ready in case anything happened.

'As a Genin, I won't be able to get my hands on anything confidential. Especially something involving Orochimaru, who seemed to cause great worry within the village. Going dark alleys, and staying too long in deserted places with no one around isn't a good idea for some time until this thing passes.'

...

As the next day came about, Shinji, like always, was in the training grounds first with Yamato. Though unlike usual, they weren't sparring this time.

Shinji of course was doing his usual training, doing pushups and all that. Yamato was standing in a tree branch, overseeing his student and pointing out any mistakes that needed fixing. Though Shinji was a little careful on not wasting too much Chakra. "Yamato -sensei, how do you think I compare to the average Genin. Recently I heard someone say that I am good, but was that true?"

"Was it Kakashi?" Yamato asked rhetorically, already seeming to know what he was talking about. "For a Genin, you're very good. I would say that you're more than ready, and just need some practical experience. Which can be earned by going on C Rank Missions."

Shinji nodded. He was a good Genin, for his rank he was good. But that wasn't the place he wanted to stand for long. His ambition wasn't to sit lazily in a comfortable place for the rest of his life. "Do you know anyone good with a sword? Maybe they can help me a little."

Yamato smiled. "Well, I might not be the best sword user out there. But I used to be in Anbu, and know a couple of shinobi who are good at it. Also, soon I should be able to convince a wind style user to come and teach you."

Shinji was glad, since just like with most things in life he wasn't talented with the sword. But sometimes hard work can trump geniuses, how many times faster does a talented person learn? 2x, 3x, or more? Then you just have to work many times harder than him and you'll surpass the genius. To Shinji this wasn't some grand saying or anything, just a simple mathematical solution of how hard work can surpass talent. Though there were exceptions to that rule too.

"By the way, sensei, when will the Chunin Exams come around this time?" Inquired Shinji, the Chunin Exams were always a big deal. But it was such a secret event that unless the finals came around, no civilian would know that the exam was happening.

"That's something that isn't allowed to be revealed right until it comes," Yamato clarified, and Shinji sighed in disappointment. But the jonin smirked. "But you need eight officially completed missions to be applicable for the Chunin Exam."

Shinji instantly caught the hint. 'We have officially completed eight D Rank missions. So that means that the Chunin Exams are quite close. If I was to try a guess, maybe around a month? Yeah, that would also correlate somewhat with the finals the years before.'

Yamato smiled at Shinji, and the genin smirked back. Both understand what had been hinted at. Still, Shinji was a little cautious in entering as his teammates weren't at his level. Of course, he didn't mean to sound arrogant and would never say this to them as an insult. But that was the truth, Sayuri and Kota couldn't keep up.

"Yamato -sensei, I think we should start working a little more in our teamwork, at least for a month," suggested Shinji. While his teammates were a little weak, that didn't make them useless as in a fight anything would help. Even a kunai thrown at the right time could change a fight's results.

Still, Shinji suggested this also had the effect of confirming to his jonin teacher that he understood the rough timeline when the Chunin Exam would happen.

"That's what I was thinking too, one month is perfect," Yamato nodded in confirmation, essentially telling Shinji that he had calculated the time perfectly of when the Chunin Exam was going to happen. "Kota and Sayuri will also be ready for a C Rank in another week or so."

"Yo! Yamato -sensei! Shinji!" Kota's loud voice permeated through the training grounds as he excitedly ran towards them with a huge smile on his face. He then saw the new sword Shinji was carrying and his eyes shone like stark. "Woah!! That looks cool as hell! Can I try it?"

Shinji shrugged, seeing no reason to stop him. "Just make sure to not cut off your hand or something."

"Oy! I am not that stupid~" Kota whined jokingly. "As long as I don't cut my middle leg, then everything else is okay."

As soon as he said that, a small stone hit Kota on the head. "Ow!" he winced, looking angrily towards where the stone came from and saw a cold-eyed Yamato. "I don't wanna hear those kinds of jokes when Sayuri is around, am I understood?"

"Sorry, Yamato -sensei," Kota was quick to apologize, with the perfect 90-degree bow. "Won't ever do this again."

He then took Shinji's sword and gaped at the weight of the sword. Shinji smiled and started giving his friend some simple instructions. "Be careful, try an overhead slash, but keep in mind that swordsmanship is more about the back muscles than you think-"

But Shinji was surprised, as this was likely the first time Kota had a sword in his hand, and probably the first time he swung a sword too. But the arc was perfect, creating a gleam, and the sound of cutting the air was something that had taken Shinji around ten minutes to get the hang of.

Now overall, that might not sound impressive to some, but the instinctual understanding of how to use a sword wasn't something that could be learned. There was only one word that describes this... talent.

Shinji was overjoyed and felt excitement burst out of his heart, they had finally found something that Kota was good at. Even Yamato had a wide-eyed look when they saw this.

"YES!" Yelled out Shinji in happiness, this freaked out Kota. Most teammates would be jealous that their teammates were talented at something, but Shinji wasn't like that and was glad that he had a teammate who could help against fights.

Shinji understood that this might have been just due to luck that Kota was able to do this for the first time. But with a smile on his face, he instructed his friend on how to get a handle on swordsmanship.

Yamato smiled, seeing Shinji who was so willing to help. But also, Kota's talent with a sword, the young genin barely had talent in anything else. No, he was barely above the average ninja, even passing the Academy Exam must have been hard. So he was quite un-talented, even though he had ambition.

But now this changed, even Yamato in his long years as a jonin showed a surprised expression as Kota got the basics of Kenjutsu down easily. "If he had half the talent he does with a sword into other things. He would be giving even Shinji a hard time."

Shinji's eyes on the other hand shone as if he had found a diamond and thanked all the gods out there if they even existed for having him pick a sword as a weapon. "Good, Kota! You've already surpassed me that has trained the basics for a whole hour and you did so in just ten minutes. As long as you work hard, with a sword, you will cut a path to your dream."

Kota stood there, looking at Shinji as if he had grown a second head. Then finally his mind seemed to comprehend what his friend had just said and tears welled up in his eyes. "Shinji... am I good at something?"

'Though he always shows a happy face and smiles. He must have been worried about his progress and lack of Chakra.' Contemplated Shinji, as the smile on his face widened and he gave his friend a thumbs up. "You're not just good, but you're so damn talented with a sword that it makes me look dumb when using it."

Kota tried to wipe away his tears, but more kept spilling out and snot covered his nose. "Shinji, I think I am crying out of happiness and can't stop. Damn... I will finally be able to stand by your side. We will be called the Demon Sword Brothers of the Setting Dark Sun Overshining The Moon."

Shinji's smile slipped off his face, and he cringed. "That name..."

"Did I miss something?" Sayuri arrived and looked on weirdly, seeing a crying Kota whose sleeves of his shirt were covered in snot and tears as he tried to wipe them away. With a cringing Shinji, and a proud Yamato looking on. "What's going on here?"

Shinji smiled at her words. "I am just thinking of destroying everyone in the Chunin Exam, I and Kota are gonna make a name for ourselves out there."

As he said that, Shinji contemplated how he should spend this week and when it would be the best time to take a C Rank Mission. Yamato seemed insistent in taking one and Shinji agreed too, but when would it be the best time?

'How hard should I work this coming week?'

_____

[Pick one and put your choice in a comment down below.]

A - Train Ninjutsu, Taijutsu, Genjutsu, and Teamwork too. Of course, sparring with Kota now too, as your talented teammate will help your Kenjutsu (swordsmanship) get better faster and push you further. This will be very hard work, but Shinji is willing to give it his all.

B - Train just Ninjutsu, Taijutsu, and Teamwork. Since Kota was already talented at Kenjutsu, you decide to try and corporate that into the team. It's hard work, but Shinji believes he can handle it.

C - Train just Ninjutsu and Kenjutsu (swordsmanship) with Kota. Send the whole week sparring against your best friend and pushing each other to be better and stronger. Hard work, but not enough to make Shinji feel intimidated.

D - Train just Taijutsu with Guy. Get your strength, speed, and stamina up to levels you would feel safe. Not that hard, and Shinji won't have to work too hard, to the point of Chakra Exhaustion.

_____

P.S: If you like the story, give it some power stones.

Chapter 15: Chapter 15 - We Stay Hungry, we Devour 3

[X] - Train Ninjutsu, Taijutsu, Genjutsu, and Teamwork too. Of course, sparring with Kota now too, as your now talented teammate will help your Kenjutsu (swordsmanship) get better faster and push you further. This will be very hard work, but Shinji is willing to give it his all

_____

Chapter 15 - We Stay Hungry, we Devour

...

A week can pass quite fast when you're training so hard you have no free time and need to keep yourself concentrated for sixteen hours a day. Shinji felt a little tired, even though he slept eight hours and ate very healthy food.

He stood in the training ground, with a sword in his hand, and he felt distracting thoughts fill his mind but he pushed through when he saw another figure with a similar sword in his hand charge towards him.

Clang! Clang! Clang!

The sound of swords clashing rang out. Shinji and Kota were sparring as the smell of wet steel filled the air. It was clear who was faster and who was more skilled, Shinji was overwhelmingly faster than Kota, his sword barely anything more than a flash to his friend.

Still, Kota had his eyes open wide like an owl, not even daring to blink at such a distance. His swordsmanship had improved massively. Since he had discovered that he was talented in something, the amount of hours he put training into it was quite a lot and would make others throw up just thinking about it. Of course, someone like Shinji was an exception to that, he would even find the work Kota was putting in kind of lacking.

Kota jumped back and put his sword into its sheath. His sword was similar to Shinji's being a Chukoto style sword, like a straight katana. Taking a deep breath, and blinking, Kota's gaze sharpened.

<Sun Sword Style: Leaping Tiger>

Chakra gathered into his legs and sword, and he leaped forward and breakneck speeds, that to any average Genin it would seem like a flash. But to Shinji... Kota was kinda slow, and he had the time to contemplate whether to block or not and decided to test his friend's strength.

CLANG!

Their swords clashed, and the sound of steel clashing rang out through the forest. Kota used both hands to hold his sword, but Shinji needed only one to block. The Sun Sword Style was one of the countless swords styles, usually used by samurais, that Yamato had been able to get his hands on and teach Kota.

"It's kinda unfair that I am bigger than you, yet physically weaker," complained Kota, judging by his words alone many would assume he might be jealous of his friend. But Shinji knew by the gleeful look on his face, Kota wasn't the guy who would bother with things like envy or jealousy. They both knew the reason he was stronger.

Shinji smirked jokingly. "It's the difference in time spent training."

"Yeah, I know, I actually have a life outside of training," Kota tried to get a rise out of his friend, but it was useless as Shinji's face was like a stone mask with a smirk etched into it. "Also, where are your Jutsu? Am I attacking so fast that you didn't have time to use them? Hehehe~ I guess-"

His words stopped mid-sentence when he saw multiple Shinji's coming from behind trees. Kota's face went from a happy one to a sigh. "This is so cheating. When did you even make them?"

"When you blinked and were about to use Leaping Tiger. At that speed you can't see clearly," Shinji explained to his friend. "So better be careful using that attack in a real battle."

Kota nodded, with a grateful look in his eyes. "True, unless you're around I won't use it against someone until my eyes get used to moving at that speed. Also, I think it would be a good idea when we fight against someone to have me use my big body to cover their view from looking at you, and then you can secretly use a jutsu without them knowing."

"That's a good idea," Shinji agreed, the smirk turning into a smile. "So, what are you going to do now?" He asked Kota Using his free hand to make a hand sign which caused the water clones to start going through hand seals. "If you jump back you'll be hit by the jutsu, if you stay close... the same ending really."

"You cheat-like bastard, can't you go easy on your talentless friend?" crocodile tears rolled down Kota's face like rivers. "I thought we were best friends."

Though his act didn't last long as they both started chuckling. Even as their swords clashed and Kota was barely able to defend some slashes, they still didn't let the sparring ruin their mood.

"Can you guys stop messing around? This is a spar, not a talk show," Sayuri's voice rang out as the surroundings around them twisted. But Shinji, having already predicted this, pulsed his chakra and dispelled the genjutsu, his surroundings going back to normal.

"Damn it," she swore under her breath. "Can't you at least act like you're having a hard time."

Shinji didn't say anything but his clones acted, half of them attacking Kota while the others went to find Sayuri's location.

[Water Style: Water Bullet] x8

Eight of his water clones spewed out orb-shaped projectiles and seeing the speed of the attack brought a confident smile to Kota's face. "Too slow," he remarked, getting into position to stop the water projectiles, having already dodged some. "Almost forgot that the water clones can only use weaker variations of your jutsu and got scared for nothing there."

"There is a reason why they are so slow," Shinji added, going through multiple hand seals in less than two seconds and his chest expanded almost unnaturally as he took a deep breath.

Kota's eyes widened, realizing what was happening, and tried to jump back. "Shit, too late."

[Wind Style: Great Breakthrough]

Booom!

A blast of wind came out of Shinji's lips, blasting trees and almost uprooting trees, grass was easily ripped out of the ground. But what surprised Kota was that the water projectiles that were slow and had almost missed him changed direction with the wind jutsu and became deadly fast.

Using his sword he was still able to cut a couple of the water projectiles, and a small splash made a cut into his shoulder and Kota noticed that the water projectiles had turned sharp, like kunai, and more powerful as he could feel his arm tingle. Kota still tried to block the water projectiles without having any of the splashes land on his body, the Sun Sword Arts that he had learned was a balanced sword style that worked well in both attack and defense.

But even then, the speed of the attacks was too much and he tried to go behind one of the trees.

poof

One of the water projectiles turned to a smiling Shinji.

Kota flipped off the Shinji that had transformed from the water projectile. "You suck. Sayuri too, where is her support? Her Genjutsus are useless against you."

But another Shinji slithered behind him and pointed a kunai at his neck.

This was the real Shinji, who had moved stealthily behind him. "You did amazingly," he complimented his teammate. "If we go back a week. You wouldn't even be able to survive ten seconds against my jutsu."

Shinji was truly impressed, with the hard work Kota had put into his swordsmanship he had improved by leaps and bounds. He might have neglected other ninja arts, like ninjutsu, or even taijutsu, but his Kenjutsu had reached levels that Shinji couldn't hold a candle to if they fought only using their swords.

'He was almost able to stalemate me in a battle of swords, even though I am faster, stronger, and have more stamina than him. So this is the difference in talent.' - Shinji contemplated, and knew that if he tried to compare himself with Kota who in a week had already mastered the Basics of Kenjutsu and already moved to a special sword style.

On the other hand, Shinji technically barely had not even mastered basic swordsmanship. He knew this was also due to Kota putting in more work into Kenjutsu than him since Shinji only worked an hour or two at best in Kenjutsu. Kota on the other hand was not only more talented but also put in around seven hours in training daily, sometimes even more.

"Now to find Sayuri," Shinji muttered and let go of his friend and tried to glance around for his other teammate. She needed to be close to cast her genjutsu, but where? This had been a battle of Sayuri and Kota against him.

But Sayuri, while she wasn't neccesarly bad in close quarters combat, Shinji knew she was smart to know that even against ten of her as he could crush her easily.

"You know, if this turns into a battle of cat and mouse it will take forever," Shinji yelled out, waiting for a reply that never came. If she yelled out anything necessarily or used a Genjutsu he would discover her position.

'She is good at stealth. If she wasn't so helpful and never does anything suspicious, then I would have assumed that she was a spy by how good at hiding she is. Especially her advancement in Genjutsu, which is a little too quick to be natural in my opinion, especially sound-related Genjutsu. If she was to be a spy, then which side would she belong to? Probably Orochimaru, that guy seemed to have his fingers in a lot of pies in Konoha. Why would she end up in my team? Probably because it was surprising that we passed and expected us to fail.'

Of course, while he contemplated this, to Shinji it was all hypothetical. But in his mind, he was playing a scenario of how it would play out if she was a spy... which she isn't.

He assumed that because if she was a spy with malicious intentions then she would have done something harmful, and masked it as something unintentional. Which otherwise would make her a spy who cared for her victims, which is something ludicrous to Shinji. Still, he shook his head to get rid of such useless thoughts in the middle of battle.

Still, he felt like there was something he wasn't seeing here. But suddenly he looked towards one of the trees where he sensed one of his water clones be destroyed. This interrupted this through and he slowly walked towards where the water clone had burst and he heard a sigh when Sayuri came from behind the tree with her hands up in the air.

Shinji pointed to the ground below her feet. "You should learn another clone technique. Maybe one that creates a shadow."

The clone Sayuri winces and sighs. "Not all of us have the chakra which doesn't even feel anything creating a dozen water clones."

"Hmmm~ is that so?" Shinji glances to the side and while everything feels normal at first, his eyes narrow. "There is no sound of the wind hitting leaves from my right. You wouldn't happen to have used false surroundings and used a sound muffling Genjutsu so I can't hear or see the kunai coming from that part? But at the same time, you silenced the leaves and the sound of kunai cutting through the air."

[Wind Style: Great Breakthrough]

Booom!!

He blew a blast of air towards the part of the place that was silent, and as expected some sound of kunai clanging was heard. When he broke out of the genjutsu, he could see the kunai too and the real Sayuri standing atop a tree. "That's some good Genjutsu, I didn't even notice when it exactly started taking effect."

She shrugged. "Glad it at least somewhat tricked you this time."

Then she jumped down and this time Shinji could tell that it was the real her, as she had just stepped into one of the water clones transformed as grass. She looked down and saw the grass that had turned into a puddle of water. "It's kinda scary how you can use such basic Jutsu with such efficiency."

Shinji shrugged. "During my time in the Academy I had nothing else but basic Jutsu and for years I tried to think of different ways to use them."

Fwish!

Suddenly Shinji felt a kunai rub against his neck, at first he thought it was Sayuri who had somehow outsmarted him. But it was Yamato. "Never let your guard down, even when you have assumed that you've dealt with the enemy."

He then grabbed Shinji behind the head. "Also what are the rumors I heard that you've been pushing yourself again? Gai has been singing praises about you."

Yamato gripped Shinji's head like an ostrich egg and his expression turned ghost-like and scary. "What did I tell you about working so hard?"

"That I shouldn't," answered Shinji reluctantly with a face that said a thousand words. "So, would an apology fix everything?"

"No, I was going to let you choose the first C Rank Mission. As a gift for your progress and helping your teammates. But it seems like you don't know what's good for your body yet. It doesn't matter if you have the will if your body fails you." Yamato warns him. "Also no training during the mission, this is your last warning, Shinji. During the fight, I could tell that you got distracted. Normally you would have at least reacted when I tried to sneak up on you. But this time, you didn't even notice at all."

Shinji nodded in agreement, he had been able to tell that he was mentally fatigued, which was dangerous in battle. If he wasn't so overwhelmingly stronger than his teammates, then he would have lost the battle, with his mind wandering around so much. "Right, no training during the mission."

Yamato narrowed his dark eyes, peering into Shinji's brown pupils. "I mean it. After all the trouble I went to find you a Wind Style teacher, the least you can do is take my advice into account."

Shinji remembered the man who had taught him some wind-style jutsu. He was an Anbu, nicknamed eagle, he was like a robot, giving instruction and demonstrating the jutsu until Shinji learned it. Not strict, but seemed to be very uptight and duty-driven. He is a very unassuming guy that never even bothered to try and get to know Shinji.

Yamato's grip on Shinji's head disappears, and the jonin sighs in disappointment. "Today we will get the mission, tomorrow we will set off. Also, Kota, I will take you to the hospital to check those wounds just in case."

Kota nodded and stood up, giving the jonin a salute. "Yes sir! I will sir!" Sayuri sighed in relief, but she looked strange at the mention of the hospital and Shinji caught that slip-up.

"Sensei, I think you should keep an eye on Kota when you're at the hospital he has..." she glanced towards Shinji and smirked. "Very Shinji-like thoughts when it comes to overdoing it."

"What's that supposed to mean?" Shinji asked, taking notice that Sayuri seemed uncertain of something.

"Nothing," she claimed, staring at the ground emotionlessly for a couple of seconds before coming to her senses. "Just warning Yamato -sensei so that we don't have to deal with someone else as troublesome as you in the team."

Sayuri spoke in a joking manner, but Shinji could tell that something was bothering her. He decided to not be petty about this and as Yamato took Kota away, Shinji approached her.

"How about you show me some places where we can have some fun and relax?" he asked since he hadn't bothered doing anything like enjoying himself after graduating from the Academy.

She was brought out of her thoughts and jumped slightly in surprise, but quickly came to her senses. "Right, I forgot you're the guy without a life outside of training."

"Hey now, you're supposed to be the girl who falls for the hard-working hero," Shinji smiled, trying to get Sayuri's mind off whatever was worrying her.

"What? That's illogical, with how much you work, no girl will like you." Sayuri reported the cold hard truth. "I mean, I am your teammate and outside of teamwork training, I don't know you. You never have free time to hang out with either."

Shinji contemplated what she said and couldn't help but agree with her. He was very busy, always looking for that next step to his power. Just like last week, he had grown stronger. But outside of training and D Rank Missions, he didn't know his teammates that much.

Even Kota and Sayuri, both of who could be considered strong Genin by now, couldn't even hold a candle against him. This wasn't arrogance, just a fact. He had fought them six times this week, and in none of them, they had been able to even scratch him. They weren't even to make him use up his chakra that much.

Shinji knew that feeling arrogant because that was stupid, which was why he didn't even feel a trace of it. Why had he won? In his eyes, it was simply because he put in more hours into training than both of them combined. That's why he was stronger than them.

'By now, I have grown comfortable in growing strong and working so hard. How will things play out if I don't train hard? Will Kota surpass me? While he wasn't talented in anything ninja-related other than swords, that lone talent was enough to overshadow his lack of other talents.'

"What do you think will happen to an average joe like me if he doesn't work hard?" Shinji asked Sayuri as they walked together out of the training grounds.

"I don't know," Sayuri shrugged. "Be a normal genius?" she added. "Also, I'm taking you to a dango shop I like. You're even worse at noticing people's feelings than Kota."

"That's debatable," Shinji chuckled, remembering how Kota can sometimes be. He walked next to her, looking onto the Konoha streets somberly. "Do you know how long it took me to learn the transformation jutsu?"

"In the Academy?" she tilted her head, her finger tapping her chin as she had a thoughtful depression. "I… don't remember. Were you bad at it? Like Naruto was with the clone jutsu?"

Was? What's that supposed to mean? Was Naruto no longer bad at the Clone Jutsu? Does Sayuri know something he didn't?

Shinji wondered if he was maybe reading too much into the situation, so he dismissed it. "No, I wasn't bad at it. Neither was I good. Average, it took around three weeks for most of the class to learn it, and that's how much it took me too."

"So? Am I supposed to think less of you for that?" Sayuri pointed towards a well-decorated dango shop. "That's the place."

"No, I am not trying to make myself seem weaker, or stronger here." Shinji clarified, walking alongside her and they arrived at the relatively quiet dango shop that had almost no customers. "I am just stating my abilities. I am neither special nor talented. At best people seem to assume I am something which I am not. As soon as I stop training, that lead I have will stop too. There is no miraculous power up waiting for me at the end of the road."

Sayuri stared at Shinji for a little bit as they found a table to sit down. "I really am stupid," she sighed, seemingly having thought of something that she doesn't logically agree with. "Well, I can help you this one time. But if you go blabbering to everyone about what I am about to say, then I will kill you."

"Kill me?" Shinji raised a questioning brow. But his talk was interrupted as a waitress came along and asked for their order. "A plate of dango, please."

"Get me hiruma dango," Sayuri said with a smile. Shinji was a little confused, he knew those were expensive, but why was she buying them? She was still paying for her stuff after all.

"Anyway, Shinji, if we fought ten times, how many times do you think I would win?" she asked, a smile on her face. Shinji didn't want to sound rude or lie, so he just shrugged.

"You would win every single battle," she stated confidently, her smile widening. "I probably wouldn't even be able to make you need to try that hard. "She took a bite of the dango and her gaze turned intense. "But when it comes to killing, I can kill you while you sleep, or when you're eating, or shitting."

Shinji nodded, deciding not to say anything, but he wondered how she would act if she knew that he was always on guard ever since the whole Orochimaru fiasco. Even when he sleeps, he does so under his bed while his clone sleeps on the real thing.

'I have thought someone would attack me and contemplated how I might go and do that if I was an assassin and have taken countermeasures.'

He stared at her and nodded, not even a trace of fear in his eyes which left his teammate confused. Seeing that, to not hurt her feelings, he added. "Oh, that's scary. Anyway, what're you going to show me?"

She narrowed her eyes at him, but in the end, sighed. "Jeez, act a little afraid at least. I just threatened your life. Don't trust me too much."

'It's not necessarily like that.' - Shinji thought, but in the end decided to play along to her demands, she was after all going to show him something that is supposed to be a secret. "Ohhh~ that's terrifying."

She took a deep breath and massaged her forehead. "I can't tell if you're mocking me or not," Shinji was about to answer, but she stopped him by putting her hand up and pointing a finger at Shinji. Slowly a tendril of Chakra came out of it, it looked like a somewhat translucent string. "This is a chakra string, I can't form long ones. But essentially it's the peak of Chakra Control for Ninja. Some medical techniques have similar effects and help with Chakra Control, but this is something kind of like that, both ways you can achieve Chakra Control that few Jonin ever bother to learn."

She then explained how to do the jutsu, by usually putting a leaf on the tip of your finger and letting it fall while still attached to a thin chakra string. They didn't have leaves on hand, so she demonstrated with a dango stick.

Shinji observed the process and memorized it. He tried to do it but had no success at all, showing that the technique was something quite hard to master. But Shinji could tell the chakra control that even most Jonin didn't bother to practice, was very useful to him. Since at most, this would have 3% of Chakra used in a jutsu, and the effort put on it wasn't worth the return for most.

Still, for him, this was another opportunity to evolve. He knew that Chakra Control helped with using fewer hand signs in jutsu, and while not even Jonin would bother with such a thing, unlike old middle-aged Jonin, Shinji had the time and ambition to train like this.

"Thanks," he was grateful towards her. Grateful and suspicious as hell now. - 'Maybe that spy theory of mine might not be so wrong after all.'

"Don't question where I got the knowledge from, and don't tell anyone. Those are the promises that I want you to keep, and whenever you feel a roadblock, I will help you to the best of my abilities." Sayuri reasoned. She seemed casual when she spoke about it, but Shinji knew the risks she was taking if his theory was right, or if she somehow was the heir of some secret clan.

"So why are you going this far for me?" Asked Shinji, inspecting her face, trying to find any trace of deceit or evil intentions, there was none. "I don't mean to sound rude," he contemplated whether he should say what he was about to say. But since he was tired mentally, he didn't think about it as much as he usually would have. "But I don't think we are close enough for you to do something like this. It isn't a matter of just life and death either."

"I said, don't ask questions," her eyes sharpened.

"Okay, okay," he waved her off and looked to the side, glancing at the entrance of the shop. "Jeez, a teammate with so many secrets. How am I supposed to trust my back to you?"

"Don't worry, I won't betray you," she said smirking before getting up. "Also this dango treat is your payment to me."

She started walking off with a smug smile on her face.

"Uhhh... I don't have any money on me." Shinji's words made her stop in her tracks, she turned around, and peered at him maliciously. Her intent to kill was as clear as daylight.

"What did you just say..." she muttered angrily, giving him a chance to take his words back. But Shinji didn't want to wash plates today.

"You know, keeping money on me when it could get wet while sparring. Even storage scrolls could be destroyed." Shinji had thought about this problem quite a lot, but it didn't seem to appease Sayuri so he also added. "I don't have a lot of money, to begin with, because training weights, food, explosion tags, and ninja soldier pills too. Also leaving my wallet somewhere close by while I train, it could get stolen."

"It's the second time you made me do this," she clenched her teeth and took out a wallet, opening it revealed stacks of money, she had a lot, and she paid for both of them. "Also enjoy the rest of the day," she sighed while looking at his face, as her anger seemed to slip out of her. "Tomorrow we will set off on our first C Rank Mission."

The waitress saw this all transpire, and she frowned, coming and taking the money while whispering under her breath. "Men these days. Using women for money."

'I am twelve, lady, and stop talking behind your customer's back.'

Shinji ate the rest of his dango and thought about what to do for the rest of the day. He had until tomorrow to do something. Shinji wondered what he should do, maybe try his hand at doing something fun?

What do you even consider fun nowadays? Learning new jutsu? No, it needs to be something that doesn't involve training.

_____

[Pick one and put your choice in a comment down below.]

A - See if you can help around the orphanage you used to live in.

B - Go and play some Shogi at the park, with the old people there. Shinji knows that old people have lived many times longer than him, and might have some wisdom to give?

C - Tell Yamato, or if you can't find him, another Jonin about your suspicions of Sayuri. Shinji knows that this will betray his teammates' trust.

D - Go train Chakra Strings and try to get the hang of it. Shinji feels kind of tired of that, having worked like mad for over three weeks straight now. But maybe he can try one last time? Shinji hopes Yamato - sensei won't catch wind of this.

E - Give Sayuri that dinner that you promised. You've stood her up twice and made her pay for your things. So take her out for dinner. (Trait: Multitasking in effect) Since dinner is quite a bit away, maybe you can also have the option to go and talk to play Shogi with some old folk at the park?

_____

Author Note:

Jesus, he rolled so well on figuring out Sayuri's identity. Also, be careful when not listening to people's advice, Shinji could have chosen a C Rank Mission. But due to Yamato's advice being ignored to take it easy on the training, then he will choose for us.

P.S: If you like this story, don't forget to give it some power stones.

Chapter 16: Chapter 16 - Put in the Work, Put in the Hours... to be normal.

E - Give Sayuri that dinner that you promised. You've stood her up twice and made her pay for your things. So take her out for dinner. (Trait: Multitasking in effect) Since dinner is quite a bit away, maybe you can also have the option to go and talk to play Shogi with some old folk at the park?

————

Chapter 16 - Put in the Work, Put in the Hours... to be normal.

...

After getting his second meal paid for by Sayuri, Shinji decided to repay this debt to her. But until dinner, it was hours away and Shinji wondered where he should take her. First and foremost, he didn't have the kind of money to take her somewhere fancy.

He followed after Sayuri, as she walked out. Shinji noticed the waitress looking on with an excited look on her face.

'Jeez, woman, do your job and stop prying so much into your customers' private lives.'

Still, he decided to ignore the waitress and called out to Sayuri. "Hey! Are you free tonight?"

Turning around she looked at Shinji weirdly at first, but immediately realized what was happening and she nodded. "Yes, I am."

She then suddenly walked off, well, more like jumped off as she started roof hopping. Faster than usual, if Shinji didn't know any better he would think that she was excited.

"I didn't even tell her the time or place we will meet at," muttered Shinji, wondering what had gotten into her. But he dismissed such thoughts, and instead contemplated on what to do until waiting for dinner time to come around.

Suddenly he smiled, remembering that there was a park, where elderly men and women met up to play Shogi against each other. Unlike most kids his age, if it wasn't something that had to do with training, Shinji wasn't sure of what to do in his free time. So he decided to go and get a look at the place.

...

Since it was close by, it didn't take long to reach the place. It was a small park, with tables set about and elderly people playing Shogi and many other games against each other, with green trees surrounding the area, and the fresh air permeating the atmosphere. Shinji stood by the sidelines, not knowing what to do at first until he saw an old man with a Konoha headband. He was too old to be a ninja, so Shinji could only assume that he only wore the headband to reminisce about the old days.

"Excuse me," Shinji said while walking closer, making sure to keep his posture neutral and have his face seem as friendly as always. "Is this place free?"

"It's a public place kid, I don't own it," said the old man, a smirk making its way into his old face which caused his wrinkles to become more etched.

Shinji stared at the man and smiled slightly. "That was a bad joke, old man."

The old man ran a hand over his spiky white hair and chuckled. "Jeez, brats nowadays keep getting more and more mouthy. Back in my days, just to go to the academy you had to walk through five enemy chunin a day."

As the old man continued explaining how he once stumbled into Madara's fight against Hashirama as a kid, Shinji decided to only half-listen to the story. The reason for that was because the chances of it being a lie were quite high.

After setting the shogi pieces down, the old man mentioned toward the neatly organized table. "I will let you move first as a sign of new friendship between the old and the new generation."

"I don't know how to play shogi," Shinji confesses, with an emotionless look on his face. "I came just to observe the place and see what I could do. Not even half an hour ago was when I decided to try this out."

The old man sighed out loudly. "Young people nowadays. Where did your manners go?"

"Cmon now, old man, I am sure that you remember a couple of rude and annoying people in your time." Shinji smiled towards the old man.

His words caused the old man to smirk. "Let's play the game now. What should I call you again?"

"Shinji, just Shinji."

"Oh? So an orphan then? That's not surprising, the Nine-Tails Attack killed your parents? Or something else?"

"No, it was the Nine-Tails Attack, I never knew them. Though I do know due to some documents that they were just some average civilians." Shinji stated calmly. He never even knew his parents, so he wasn't that affected by their death, and he had twelve years to get used to the feeling too."What about you old man, what's your story?"

"My story? It's even more boring than yours," he chuckled but hurriedly added. "I meant no offense to you by saying that."

"None taken."

"I was born in an era where the villages didn't exist. Things were so bad that it made Ninja Wars seem like child's play. There was always constant fighting and wars." He gazed down with a sad gaze in his eyes. "I used to have a son about your age during the second ninja war."

Shinji didn't say anything when he heard that, he didn't know what to say either. He wasn't experienced with situations like these. The old man's sad look turned into a smile as he glanced at Shinji. "Anyway, let me explain the rules of Shogi."

...

Hours later, Shinji was sitting at the same table, and the old man stood opposite of him and he had a smirk on his face. "Hey~ make your move. An old man like me might die before you get to make yours."

Shinji could see that no matter what he did, he would lose two movies later and he wasn't pleased with that. But for the first time in a while, he wasn't thinking about just training and was trying to think of a strategy.

"You're a smart kid," the old man complimented him. "But you sacrifice pieces too easily. Think of them as real people, as your teammate and you'll rack your brain trying to think of strategies to not have them destroyed."

Shinji nodded and tried to think of it like that. Sadly, he didn't have too many people that he cared about... or even ones he called friends to fill the roles in the pieces. Still, he took the old man's advice.

...

As the sun set, the old man still had an amused smile on his face. They had played many games by now, but Shinji hadn't won any of them, but he wasn't annoyed or angry. This has been a learning experience. The old man's advice had been very helpful too, as there were many situations Shinji hadn't thought of and how the experience could be taken into account.

The old man had the experience of playing Shogi, that was why even as Shinji came up with new ideas, they weren't new to the old man. That same analogy could be used for Ninja, and how sometimes an old man, who has been in hundreds of fights will do better than just some young man who knew how to think well into his feet.

'When fighting against an experienced enemy, I need to think of something that is original and they can't predict.'

Shinji contemplated just how he would go against fighting someone better, stronger, and more experienced? He... couldn't come up with an answer. At least he didn't think he would be able to overcome something like that in such a short time and on the spot. The world had all kinds of ninja with different abilities, so Shinji knew he had to keep a sharp and open mind to every possibility and how he would be able to deal with something like that.

The sun started setting, casting a shadow over the shogi board, he sighed and got up. "Seems like a loss again, how many times was this? Fifteen? Seventeen?"

"It's only thirteen times," the old man reassured him. "But you have potential at least."

"Thanks, this helped me a lot more than I thought it would," Shinji admitted, having fun was a part of human life too. Training all day would have consequences and he knew that humans weren't like rocks, and he was a human too. "Anyway, I promised someone to take her to dinner."

"Ohhh~" the old man smiled mischievously. "Go get your lady love~"

"It's not like that, old man. I am twelve and have plenty of time to find a girl I like," Shinji said while walking off, but he stopped mid-way and turned around, looking at the old man. "By the way, I never got your name."

"When you come around next time, then maybe I will tell you my name," the old man waved him off as Shinji didn't pry more into it, knowing how some ninja liked to keep their secrets.

He didn't want to be late for the date so he walked off. Though he hadn't discussed where they would meet or at what time, he went towards the entrance of the training grounds where they usually trained. As he walked there, he saw Sayuri walking towards the same place.

She smirked at him like she usually does and waved. "So you did come. I suspected that you might have forgotten."

"Jeez, just how low do you think of me? I gave you my word, so of course, I was going to come," he muttered, frowning at her.

"I am joking," she added, getting close and grabbing Shinji's arm with a smile on her face. She pouted and walked back, twirling, showing that she wasn't wearing her usual ninja clothes but a nice dress that fluttered about like a flower. "So? What do you think?"

"..." Shinji was confused at first but understood that she was talking about her dress. "It looks good," he remarked, and looked her up and down, making Sayuri blush a little. "But it also seems very inconvenient to move with. It's unnecessarily restricting," seeing the frosty expression on her face he added, "Still looks good on you though."

Sayuri sighs, but still intertwines her arm with Shinji's and whispers. "Where do you plan to take me?"

Shinji smiles confidently, not noticing the strange way she spoke those words or how she mushed her body against his. "There is a place I was introduced to recently and it has some amazing food."

Her eyes lit up at the mention of the place. "Oh? Seems like you have thought about this a lot."

...

Her expectations were crushed as soon as her excitement had reached the peak as they arrived at a rundown ramen stand. "Ichiraku Ramen?" She read the sign and looked at Shinji once more before sighing. "Well, what're you waiting for, let's go in."

She dragged Shinji in and he could see that she was disappointed and told her the truth. "Sorry if this isn't some fancy place. I don't have the money to take you somewhere better."

'Also in case the C Rank fails tomorrow, I don't want to be left penniless.'

Sayuri stopped, turned, and glanced at Shinji with shocked eyes at first, and then smiled appreciatively. "Don't worry, I don't mind. I just like acting like a stuck-up bitch sometimes. Though for tonight, you have to listen to a lot of my complaints about life."

"That's the least I can do."

Shinji smiled back and they walked into the small ramen stand, which had the living quarters above. Shinji assumed that the 2nd floor was where the owner lived. Ichiraku saw them and smiled widely. "Welcome! What can I get you?"

After giving their orders Ichiraku went and Sayuri immediately started talking. "Well, where should I start? Hmmm... did you know that my parents sold me away to pay off their debts?"

"That's terrible," Shinji remarked, surprised that such things still happen nowadays. He knew that Sayuri was hiding something she couldn't tell him. But people aren't just a casket of pre-set behaviors and instincts. Every one of them had something in the past that made them who they are. "Still, at least you are in a better place now."

"Am I?" She smiled bitterly, and immediately Shinji realized that something was going on that he didn't know of. He guessed that it was something that had to do with her secret, but he wasn't sure whether prying into that would be a good idea. "My parents never gave a thought about me and sold me, the buyer thought of me as a tool too. What a shitty life," a single tear rolled down her eye. "Not having someone care about you. No parent to give you a packed lunch, not a sibling, not even a damn person in the world who cares what happens to me. When I die, I'll disappear into nothing. Even the man who raised me to a useful tool probably doesn't remember my name or that I even exist. What is my life even worth-"

"I care," Shinji intervened. Looking her in the eyes. "Whether you die or live, I will remember you and so will Kota and Yamato -sensei. Whether you want to or not, you're part of our lives now and we will forever remember you."

She wiped the single tear that had rolled down and her expression went back to one of mischief, which was something Shinji was more familiar with. "Hahaha, were you tricked by my act?"

Shinji contemplated what to say, and how to act on this. His mind ran over a dozen things. But only some of them were legible.

———————————————

A - "Yes, you're quite convincing." Shinji doubted that it wasn't an act but decided to not call her out on it. Seeing that she had her reasons to hide it. Shinji suspects that Sayuri might see through this answer and understand his real thoughts on the situation.

B - "If you ever need help with something, then I will be there for you." Shinji didn't answer whether he believed her act or not and just wanted her to know that she wasn't alone.

C - "That's not an act and we both know it." Shinji is afraid this might sound rude to her, and ruin their relationship.

D - "I think we should be honest with each other and try to get you out of this situation. I will help you, Sayuri." Shinji doesn't know how this might play out, but he will try and get Sayuri out of this horrible situation. "I can only help you by knowing what is going on."

E - "..." Don't say anything and just wait for the ramen. Shinji hopes the ramen comes soon or the situation could turn awkward very soon.

P.S: If you like the story, don't forget to give it some power stones.

Join discord where I post the dice rolls of the chapter and their effects.

Discord:

https://discord.gg/wbwRTqd7jr

Chapter 17: Chapter 17 - C Rank Mission

B - "If you ever need help with something, then I will be there for you." Shinji didn't answer whether he believed her act or not and just wanted her to know that she wasn't alone.

_____

Chapter 17 - C Rank Mission

...

Shinji contemplated how to try and approach this situation, there wasn't necessarily a right way to approach a situation like this. But he wanted to reassure Sayuri of one thing first. "If you ever need help with something, then I will be there for you."

Her eyes widened at the words, she then looked towards the table, hiding her face from Shinji, so he couldn't tell what she was thinking. "That's such a cringe thing to say," she muttered. "You don't know about what's happening behind the scenes and you want to try helping me?"

He didn't back down due to her words and shrugged, giving her as much of a non-answer as he could without sounding like he wasn't on her side. Helping her? Well, he didn't know the situation and was cautious to get into something unknown. But helping her to the best of his abilities, as long as it wasn't something outrageous? Of course, he would. She was his teammate after all.

Shinji had his suspicions of what her situation was, and that same feeling of suspicion had been getting stronger lately, especially since Sayuri acted as if she would die soon. But he crushed such feelings by willpower alone, knowing that such things would only bring chaos to the team. "I will help you and have your back, as your teammate, that's my duty."

She smiled, glancing at him and the happy look in her eyes. "You're so logical, but during times like these you're quite soft."

"Not necessarily. You're someone who I want to trust my back to, if I am in a life or death situation, I wish you would have my back. So of course, I can't expect you to do the same for me, if I don't reciprocate." Shinji explained his reason, he knew that there might come a day when his life is in danger, and when it did, he didn't want to have Sayuri or Kota leave him behind. Rather, he would like it if they helped him, and he would do the same if they ended up in a desperate situation.

Sayuri turned to look at Shinji, and she had a smile on her face while gazing at him and he couldn't quite decipher what she was thinking. Her blue eyes peered into his brown ones and she chuckled. "Then don't worry, I will have your back," she got up and glanced at a shop nearby. "I'm going to get us some drinks until the ramen comes. What an amazing teammate you have, isn't that right?"

She didn't wait for an answer and just got up, going to buy the drinks. Shinji stared at her as she walked away and sighed. During these weeks he had spent training doing something he found easier than talking to teammates.

As his mind wandered, he saw Ichiraku, the middle-aged man who had his usual smile on and brought the ramen. "Enjoy!" he gave Shinji a thumbs up with a knowing look. "By the way, since you're my 50,000th customer, you'll get this meal for free! Congratulations!"

"Thanks," Shinji thanked the man, glad to not have and waste money on it. But as he thought about the situation, he couldn't help but think that something was strange. Why would the old guy give away free meals to him? Shinji didn't believe himself to be that lucky.

But as he was thinking that, Sayuri came in with two unopened drinks, it was apple juice.

'Right, and just as she was away, I miraculously no longer have to pay for the meals. Also if we were really his 50,000th customer, then Ichiraku would have announced it as soon as we came in, not now as he brought the food. That's how it usually goes.'

He thought about how Sayuri went to buy drinks and the shop's distance, unless there was a small line, it wouldn't have taken this long. Also from what he observed, there were only a couple of customers in the other shop.

'Well, it seems like this is the third time she pays for my meal. So she probably used the buying drinks as an excuse to go and pay Ichiraku for the meal and give some lame excuse. Must have been worried about my finances...'

Shinji decided to not say and act like he didn't notice what she did. "It seems like my luck took a turn for the better. The meal is free due to being the 50,000th customer."

"What?" Sayuri pouted. "Now you have to take me out again after our C Rank Mission. Because this doesn't count."

Shinji chuckled at her words and nodded. "Sure," he had no reason to refuse as he might just get another free meal on top of getting to know his teammate better. "Maybe next time we should invite Kota too."

The sour expression that came to Sauri's face as soon as those words left his mouth was a clear indication of her feelings on the matter. Shinji smirks, amused at her sudden change in demeanor.

...

During the rest of the evening, their conversation went normally and it was mostly light-hearted.

Shinji went to his apartment, which now looked like it belonged to a ninja. The windows were trapped and a couple of genjutsu were woven as soon as he entered. Like always, he took out a futon and put it under his bed, while making a water clone and having it sleep in his real bed.

Staring at the wooden beams that held his mattress, from under his bed, Shinji smiled. "Today wasn't so bad. Maybe I should relax more often like this."

For the first time in a while, Shinji wasn't so tired that when his head hit the pillow he would fall asleep. Instead, he had some time to himself and think about how much he had changed after graduation.

...

The next day came by fast, as if in the blink of an eye, and Shinji was relaxed, with a smile on his face as he got up and smelled the fresh morning wind flowing through his window. He had never felt so relaxed, his mind was sharp like a razor, and his body wasn't fatigued at all.

Which was new to him, even though it had been just three weeks of such hellish training, the sensation of being well-rested felt so new to him.

With a smile on his face, he went to the bathroom and looked at himself in the mirror, brown eyes stared right back at him with slightly spiky dark hair dripping slightly along his face. Shinji smiled and started doing his morning routine.

He put on his usual clothes, he had many pairs of the same clothes. Humans wasted a lot of thought processes even picking something as simple as their clothes. During his training weeks, Shinji couldn't waste time like that and just had sleeveless gray hoodies with dark short-sleeved shirts and dark pants with ninja sandals.

Today was a special day as Yamato had told them to prepare for the C Rank Mission, and Shinji had prepared adequately for it. He took a small backpack that was filled with storage scrolls that had food, medicine, survival kits, and other things. Though he had two scrolls full of water, just in case he was running low on Chakra and needed to have some surrounding water.

..

Unlike usual, where they would meet in the training grounds, today Shinji was early like always and waited for them just outside of the Hokage Tower. Not long after him, Yamato appeared and he waved at Shinji with a happy smile on his face. The jonin no longer seemed to be angry about Shinji previously not listening.

From what Shinji could tell, his jonin teacher seemed somewhat happy. "You seem happy today?"

"Of course I am," Yamato stated proudly, ruffling his student's hair. "My Genin are finally going to become a fully-fledged ninja."

"Sensei!" Kota yelled out as he ran towards them with a big backpack. Both Shinji and Yamato stared at him dully, as if he was doing something stupid. Kota tilted his head in confusion, not understanding why they were looking at him like that. "What's wrong?"

Shinji suddenly noticed something move stealthily around the trees and saw that it was Sayuri, she was moving amongst the trees quite fast. But he easily caught sight of her, even as she went behind him.

"Use storage scrolls," Sayuri advises Kota. Yamato smiled and nodded as if complementing her abilities, and agreeing with her words.

Shinji turned around and smiled at his teammate. "It looks less cool when the victim you're trying to scare already notices you. Though the way you used the shadows of the trees and Genjutsu to make yourself less visible was amazing."

sigh

She sighed in disappointment. "I will teach it to you later."

"Anyway, now that you're all here, let's go and meet Hokage -sama," Yamato brought their attention to him. "I already notified the Hokage yesterday and have just the perfect mission as the first one for you."

So with Yamato in the lead, they walked towards the tower… after Yamato lent Kato a storage scroll. Shinji contemplated if his jonin teacher had predicted something like that would happen?

…

Shinji cringed internally at the sight of the Hokage's office, it was filled with papers and even with five Chunin helping him, the Hokage was swarmed.

Was it because of the Chunin exams that were coming soon? Shinji wondered, but his mind stopped thinking of such things as the Hokage's eyes settled on him and he smiled.

"Yamato, you've come for the first C Rank mission?" Hiruzen addressed the jonin, with a grandfatherly smile on his face.

Except for the first D Rank Mission of the new Genins, the Hokage didn't usually give the rest of the D Rank missions and they were handled by other Chunin that work as paper pushers. Opening a scroll, Hiruzen glanced at Shinji and the others.

"Tanzaku Prison Escapees, C Rank, many criminals imprisoned there have escaped as of recently. You will have to help the officials deal with the escaped prisoners, the payment is the highest possible for a C Rank Mission, at 100,000 Ryo." Hiruzen continued reading the rest of the contents in the scroll, which included contents of where the prisoners might have escaped, eye-witnesses, and how there were some suspicions that they had formed a group of mountain bandits. After finishing reading the scroll, the Hokage threw it at Yamato, and the jonin caught it. "Normally, for new Genin as their first mission it is an Escort Mission, but Yamato has insisted that you're ready for this. Be careful out there."

After saying that, everyone nodded respectfully towards the Hokage and walked out of the office of the busy village leader. Shinji was glad that he didn't have to deal with things like this at least. Though he likes studying Jutsu and is curious about any Secret Techniques, Konoha might have. Becoming Hokage to get his hands on that sounded like a pain.

Still, Shinji was quite ambitious in getting his hands on some rare jutsu, knowing that without them he at best will reach some Jonin level. He needed to be special in some way or another.

…

The road to Tanzaku was quite far away and would take days to travel to. Even as ninjas, they could at most lower that time in a day or so. Because they also had to take into account saving stamina, and being ready for surprise encounters.

As team 13, they weren't specialized in tracking or anything like that. A team set to fail, without a specialization. But as they moved through the forests, they were nothing less than a blur.

Fwish!

Shinji was on the right flank, and he was a little cautious of the mission. Yamato wasn't the kind of teacher who would deliberately pick something dangerous for them.

So he brainstormed to figure out what his teacher was getting at here.

"This mission wasn't chosen at random," Yamato suddenly announced. His voice is serious, leaving no room for debate. "While the details aren't exactly written down, the situation is a little more delicate than just taking care of the prisoners."

"What do you mean, sensei?" Kota asked nervously, as he could sense the tense situation. A bead of sweat rolled down his cheek.

Yamato continued staring forward, and after a couple of seconds of silence, he added. "You must kill the escapees. This mission was handpicked by me to give you the taste of what it feels like to kill. As a ninja, you're dancing with death every mission. I don't want you to learn what it feels to kill in a critical situation."

Shinji caught on to that while Kota seemed nervous at the prospect of having to kill someone. While Sayuri seemed perfectly calm, like always. People reacted differently when killing someone, and her reaction wasn't anything strange. Though Shinji suspected that this might not be the first time she will kill someone. But he kept that thought to himself.

While he was observing the others, he also took account of himself. How was he feeling about this? Well, Shinji felt strangely calm, initially, he had thought that this would be more nerve-wracking. But unexpectedly, he had never felt calmer. It was quite strange.

Checking his pulse, his heartbeat also was normal.

Was it because it was just words that he wasn't panicking? Or maybe ever since joining the academy, he knew that killing people is part of a ninja's job. So this didn't come as a surprise to him.

But right now, amongst all the people in his team, the person who was the biggest mystery to Shinji right now was... himself.

Still, he didn't delve into it for too long and concentrated on his surroundings. This was the first time he had been out of Konoha, and unlike back in the village, he couldn't relax out here and play around.

'Hmmm... I wonder how it will feel to kill someone? There's no avoiding it now, I have understood this for a long time now. But how will it feel when I kill someone? Will I be sad? Traumatized? Terrified? Fascinated with life? Or maybe I will not be bothered by it.'

...

Tanzaku, a town surrounded by high and thick walls. It also had a giant historical castle in the middle, which was a good tourist attraction. But even with all that, this place was mostly known for its gambling houses, casinos, and such things.

Shinji and the rest of the team walked along the streets casually. "What are we doing here?" Shinji inquired. "Don't we already have the information we need?"

"We need the updated information," Yamato explained. "Only then can we act. Also while you have the mission to take care of the prisoners, I have another mission that correlates with it. I'll explain it later."

Shinji frowned, trying to understand the situation. He didn't like now knowing something, and there was more to the mission than it seemed. Also, the prisoner's escape in and of itself was a little suspicious. The first thing that Shinji found suspicious was how long it had taken to contact the Ninja. There are cases when it happens, but that's only when some bandits take over a village and no messages are sent and only neighboring villages send the mission to Konoha, not wanting their villages to get taken over by criminals.

But here, Tanzaku Town didn't seem to be taken over at all and was even thriving. So why did it take so long for the Mission to be deployed to Konoha? The mission description said that the escapees might have even had the time to make a bandit camp in the mountains. Shinji estimated that for something like that to happen it should take at least a month.

What kind of person would let dangerous fugitives run around for a whole month? Shinji could think of hundreds of reasons. From the local noble needing a big incident to cover something else, or maybe he just wanted people to panic a little to take their gaze away from his questionable leadership.

Still, all that speculation wouldn't lead to an answer, so Shinji stopped thinking about it and instead decided to observe the situation, how it develops, and learn the truth by himself.

"You stay around here, enjoy yourself and explore the town. While I go and take care of some things with the local governor." Yamato stated, before blitzing away in a Body Flicker.

Left to his machinations, Shinji didn't know what to do. Kota seemed just as confused, but Sayuri had a devilish smirk as she glanced towards her teammates. "Shinji, you're smart right?"

"Intelligence is a relative thing," he answered. "Also in comparison to some geniuses, I would call myself normal."

"Have you ever thought of counting cards? Gambling is a good way of earning money," Sayuri tried to entice him, but Shinji stood casually as if a buddha untainted by material desire.

"Well, having some more money on hand would help with training," he nodded, which made Sayuri stare at him with a disappointed gaze.

"Is training all you think about?" she sighed.

"Counting cards? That's cheating!" remarked Kota, unwilling to partake in this.

Shinji nodded, agreeing with him. "You're right, the risks aren't worth the rewards. A Genin doing this could ruin Konoha's reputation and that will have some lasting effects on my career. For example, I might not be promoted to Chunin if I am found out to be cheating here. Because as a Chunin it will require someone to be more trustworthy than someone who uses his ninja abilities to cheat in gambling."

"Okay, okay," Sayuri nodded, trying to stop his ramblings. "How about you try legitimate gambling then," she sighed. "An honest ninja, that sounds like the punchline to a joke."

Still, Shinji was firm in his beliefs, not because he didn't want to cheat, but because of the negative impacts, it might have on his future. Unless he wanted to become a Missing Ninja, doing things that could impede your career wasn't a smart thing in his opinion.

"Geez, we are in the capital of gambling and we aren't gambling at all," Sayuri pouted. "You know, as Ninja, our lives could end at any moment. So it's normal to get some quirks or bad habits, it helps keep you sane."

Kota smiled. "Die?" he intervened in the conversation with a confident gaze. "I and Shinji aren't allowed to die until we accomplish our goals."

...

The trio spent some time as a team and acted like tourists, visiting the nearby castle, trying different foods, and talking to the locals. That lasted until Yamato returned, and Shinji also got another bit of news while talking to the locals. While the local people had heard of the prisoner's escape, it seemed like the local governor hadn't made a big deal of it and reassured the people he would get Konoha Ninja to help.

'So that dismisses my theory that the local governor is into shady business and is trying to cover it up. Or else, he would have made the news bigger and exaggerated the escapees' crimes to make people more fearful of them.'

"Yamato -sensei, what's the real mission?" Shinji glanced at his jonin teacher, Yamato sighed.

"Don't worry, your mission is as stated in the documents. Mine is a different one. Also, our targets' locations are already known, so we don't have to do any tracking."

Those simple words made it clear to Shinji that he shouldn't talk about the mission anymore and leave it at that. Still, he decided to keep his guard up, being cautious wouldn't hurt him.

...

After a while, everyone arrived at a mountain close by, but by now it had turned dark and Shinji contemplated whether they would camp. But Yamato's eyes narrowed and following his teacher's gaze, Shinji saw a wooden structure in the middle of the forest.

The structure was surrounded by walls that were made of trees, and by the look of it, Shinji could discern that it was recently built. Mostly due to the still fresh tree stumps around. "Shinji, Sayuri, Kota, I want you to go in by yourselves and deal with the situation."

Shinji swallowed, as a nervous feeling crawled down his heart. Sayuri and Kota glanced at him, there was no need for words to be spoken. They had chosen him as their leader. Shinji knew he couldn't refuse either as if Sayuri became the leader, she was a little too reckless with her life, and Kota just wasn't leader material and was unlikely to come up with a good plan.

So Shinji first took a deep breath, calming himself as his gaze turned cold. His mind immediately started working on strategies he could use in the attack. "Sayuri, Kota, make sure to follow me stealthily and only start attacking after I do. First, we must take care of the lookouts."

As a leader, Shinji led by example, he wasn't too worried about Sayuri as she seemed calm, but Kota was a whole other deal as his eyes were blinking rapidly, his breath was heavy, and his hands shook with a kunai in them.

Shinji signaled them to wait as he caught sight of one of the scouts talking about something to the other and walking back, leaving only one of them in the lookout in that direction. Shinji saw the perfect opportunity and he took action.

Fwish!

With speed no simple bandit could follow, Shinji was in front of the guard. Looking down, the man's eyes widened in shock and fear when he saw Shinji's headband. "N-"

Shinji didn't let him talk as he might have notified his colleagues. The kunai slid through the bandit's throat like butter, cutting through flesh so easily. Tears came out of the man's eyes as blood spewed out of his neck and he fell to his knees, focused on Shinji.

The genin just stared at the dying man, now he could tell how it felt to kill someone.

———————————————

[Pick one, and put your choice in a comment down below]

A - Indifferent. It was part of his job, he didn't care about it too much. People die all the time, it was only a matter of time.

B - Scared, Terrified. Seeing someone dying wasn't the biggest thing that Shinji cared about. But looking at the man's face, it was replaced by his own... Shinji didn't want to die in a horrible way like this and will make sure with everything in his power that it doesn't happen.

C - Happy. Overpowered someone weaker than yourself and dominating them. What a feeling... something that he should explore more.

D - Sad. Shinji felt sad for killing someone, what if he had a family? Or a child? Not every prisoner is guilty. The world wasn't that black and white. Shinji feels cautious of thinking like this, as it might get in the way of his duties.

———————————————

A/N: Join discord where I post the dice rolls of the chapter and their effects. And discuss with other readers about plans for Shinji:

https://discord.gg/wbwRTqd7jr

P/S: (If you like the story, give it some power stones.)

Chapter 18: Chapter 18 - First Kill

ANNOUNCEMENT:

I am currently moving to a new residence and the chapter updates will be a little off-timed and maybe not daily until January 15th.

_____

A - Indifferent. It was part of his job, he didn't care about it too much. People die all the time, it was only a matter of time. (NEW PERKS!)

_____

Chapter 18 - First Kill

...

Shinji glanced at the man, as he clawed at his neck. It was a gross sight and one that he didn't feel happy to do. But he didn't feel necessarily bad about it either.

He had more important things to take care of, like Kota being quite panicked. As his teammate, he had to be there, and not worry about a bandit's life. People made choices in their life, and they were responsible for their own choices. Shinji wasn't going to burden himself with the wrong choices other people made.

He wouldn't get used to killing, but Shinji didn't feel guilty about it either. This was a part of his job, and he had prepared to kill someone ever since in the academy, he comprehended what he was going to have to do.

Shinji signaled towards Kota and Sayuri to follow him, they did.

"Kota, calm down, follow my orders and everything will be alright," Shinji commented calmly. "You trust me right? Remember we are the Demon Sword Brothers of the Setting Dark Sun Overshining The Moon."

Staring at his friend acting so casually, Kota seemed to relax too and take a deep breath. His eyes sharpened too, showing that he was now ready to kill too. "Sorry, I feel better now. Also as you said, that name kinda sticks now."

Shinji cringed, and this made Sayuri chuckle. The lighthearted mood calmed Kota and he stared towards one of the bandit guards. He swallowed in fear and clenched his kunai. Getting up, he calmly walked towards the bandit.

With a clean swipe, Kota's kunai cut someone's neck from behind and the bandit's body slumped to the ground. His eyes were wide in shock as his body shook while bleeding.

Sayuri went through some hand seals, and just as the man was about to scream, no sound came out of the now paralyzed bandit.

Clang

Kota's kunai clattered on the ground as he stared at his now bloody hands. Sayuri frowned. "What's that fool doing now?"

Fwish!

Shinji moved within an instant and covered Kota's mouth as they both stared at the dying man. Cutting the man on the back of his neck wasn't a good idea as it caused a bad decapitation, and Shinji could tell that it was horrible and this would visit Kota's nightmares for a while.

'This could grow to become a troublesome situation.' - thinks Shinji, using his hand to keep Kota's mouth shut so he doesn't notify the bandits with any sounds. "Kota, remember, these guys aren't good people."

Now Shinji understood that while he had thought of killing someone for years now, Kota was the exact opposite. He hadn't thought of killing anyone until the brink of when he had to do it and they came to the bandit camp.

Deciding to finish this by himself, Shinji instructed Kota to stay quiet as he moved towards the roofs of one of the crudely built houses.

There were five more bandits left, and Shinji moved around like a ghost, slitting everyone's throats without thinking about it too much. But he made sure to leave one alive for Sayuri.

The one who was left alive was a chubby man who looked around fearfully. "Who-" but his face morphed into one of terror when Shinji walked out of the shadows he was hiding.

Focusing on the Konoha headband, the man's legs buckled. "N -Ninja!!"

Fwish!

A kunai was thrown, and it pierced the man's head. Sayuri walked next to Shinji. "Heh, human lives are really easy to take."

Her comment made Shinji side-glance at her. "Be careful about what you say out loud. You've been growing reckless as of lately."

"Sorry not everyone can be as sharp-minded as you constantly," she sighed, but noticing Shinji's serious demeanor, she rubbed her eyes. "Sorry about that. I have been a little stressed out lately."

Shinji only stared at her for a couple of seconds before nodding. "Just be careful."

Fwish!

That was when the wind shifted and Yamato appeared, he looked around, seeing the dead people. He only glanced at Shinji and Sayuri for a split second, before his eyes settled on Kota. Who was staring at the dead bandit's body that he had killed.

Yamato also caught sight of the fat bandit that Sayuri had killed and the jonin went and put his dead body in a scroll. "This one messed with the wrong people." Yamato looked up at Shinji. "He sexually assaulted the governor's daughter. A father unable to deliver the death sentence to the one who killed his daughter decided to orchestrate certain events to happen."

Shinji immediately caught on to what Yamato was getting at here. Since he had asked a lot of questions about the B Rank Mission, it seemed like Ninjas were quite accommodating to the less legal side of things too.

'Yamato -sensei's B Rank Mission was probably something along the lines of making sure that the man Sayuri killed is dead. No matter what. An assassination order was made by an angry father. No doubt the Mayor made sure that the prisoner's life was so bad in prison that at any chance he would escape from there.'

Shinji didn't even want to think about this situation too much, as it was annoyingly complicated. Still, he now understood what kind of scumbags he was dealing with. "Yamato -sensei, can you explain to Kota that the people he killed were scumbags? This would help him come to terms with his actions."

Yamato nodded and immediately went to console Kota. While Sayuri observed them from afar together with Shinji.

"He is an attentive teacher," she commented, smiling slightly. "Though for your training maniacal tendencies, it's probably torture."

"That joke is getting old real fast," Shinji commented, smiling at her pouting face. Her blue eyes though showed that she was quite entertained.

...

Yamato took care of Kota and gave him as much advice as he could. Shinji couldn't hear exactly what was being said between them, but the young genin seemed to end up in a better mood. At least he wasn't panicking all over the place.

The jonin then came towards Shinji and pointed towards the buildings. "Check them all out and make sure no one is alive. If there is, kill them."

Fwish! Fwish!

Immediately both Shinji and Sayuri went searching through the houses. He found a man with dark hair, and blue eyes hiding under the bed in fear. He was middle-aged, and in his younger years might have even been handsome. But now he has scars all over his face and seems like a hardened criminal. Though as soon as he caught sight of Shinji's headband, he was so afraid he didn't even offer any resistance as Shinji slit his throat.

Sayuri didn't have better luck either. "There was no money, these bandits were poor as hell."

"Hey now, I am supposed to be the broke one here," Shinji remarked jokingly.

She put her arm around his neck in a friendly manner and chuckled along. "Yes, I know, and I am your-"

"Free meal ticket," Shinji added without missing a beat.

She stood there, frozen as if the coldest winds had hit her for a hundred years. When what he said finally registered in her mind, Sayuri's expression resembled that of a cat ready to scratch its victim.

But Shinji wasn't the kind of guy who would give an advantage and had already taken off when she was absentmindedly staring into empty space.

"Yamato -sensei, I eliminated another person, he was hiding under the bed," Shinji said respectfully, acting like he didn't notice Sayuri wanting to punch his head off, but couldn't do so due to the jonin in the vicinity.

...

Shinji made sure that he wasn't outside of Yamato's view. His actions made the knit of Sayuri's forehead grow tighter and tighter. Through all of this, the subject of her annoyance was supporting their other teammate.

Though by now he wasn't sure if she was still annoyed. As Sayuri's previous predatory smirk had turned into an amused one as she tried to get her clutches on Shinji.

"Did you get a boost in speed every time you annoy me?" She whispered, but her frown slowly morphed into a smile. "Seems like we now have the average teammate relationship. We should do this more often."

Shinji only looked at her weirdly, wondering if she is one of the people who are into things like humiliation, anger, etc? Was that considered masochism? He didn't know enough on the matter, so he didn't think too much about it.

After arriving at Tanzaku, a shadow clone of Yamato went to make a report to the governor. While this was considered unprofessional, especially for a jonin, the real Yamato was there to comfort Kota and about what he had done. Shinji was there to help too, and Sayuri looked on from the sidelines with a small smile and strange look in her eyes.

After some time in Tanzaku Town, Team 13 set off towards Konoha, with their mission completed.

"Since the Chunin Exams are so close, only two weeks away and we don't have enough time for the Chunin Exams," Yamato announced, and Shinji immediately knew that this was because of Kota, but didn't say anything as he didn't want to ruin the team dynamics.

Still, now that he knew the exact timeline, Shinji wondered what he would do with these two weeks.

"By the way, you're going to join the Chunin Exams, right?" he looked at Shinji, knowing that whatever he said, both Sayuri and Kota would follow along.

_____

[Pick one choice, and write it in the comment section below.]

A - "Yes," Shinji planned to join and get the rank of Chunin as soon as possible. He will train moderately hard during these two weeks as he plans to spend some time with his teammates to make sure they're all for the Chunin Exams.

B - "Yes, I can't wait for it," Shinji will work extremely hard, just like the three previous weeks. Though this will leave him with very little time with his teammates, and Kota might become something unpredictable in the exam.

C - "No, maybe next time. We aren't ready yet." Shinji felt like Sayuri's strange reactions and Kota's recent shock would make them an unstable team.

D - "No," Shinji answered simply, as he felt like he wasn't strong enough for the Chunin Exams yet.

_____

Author Note/ ANNOUNCEMENT:

I am currently moving to a new residence and the chapter updates will be a little off-timed and maybe not daily until January 15th.

P.S: If you like the story, give it some Power Stones.

P.P.S: Join discord where I post the dice rolls of the chapter and their effects. And discuss with other readers about plans for Shinji:

https://discord.gg/wbwRTqd7jr

Chapter 19: Chapter 19 - Chunin Exam Rumble

A - "Yes," Shinji planned to join and get the rank of Chunin as soon as possible. He will train moderately hard during these two weeks as he plans to spend some time with his teammates to make sure they're all for the Chunin Exams.

_____

Chapter 19 - Chunin Exam Rumble

…

Two weeks passed in the blink of an eye for Shinji and his team. This time, unlike before, Shinji wasn't the only one who worked hard. As a team, their bond became something unshakable, and an unbreakable belief in battle had formed between them. Now Shinji was confident that if it came down to it, his team would have his back, no matter what.

Kota had also somewhat closed the gap that had been created in his skills due to him physically being unable to keep up with his swordsmanship. Now he had grown into someone Shinji could count on in a tight situation. Having discovered his swordsmanship talent had reassured Kota that as long as he worked hard, his dream of becoming an S Rank ninja was within reach.

But even with the progress he made, the one Shinji was surprised by is Sayuri. For some reason, she started working hard like her teammates. Her improvements in such a short time were something that even Shinji wasn't sure he could match, at least in Genjutsu.

Her talent in the Illusionary Arts had also shown itself, as even Yamato commented that her Genjutsu was something that most Chunin would be unable to break through or even notice.

Overall, it had been a fruitful two weeks.

Initially, Shinji had been unsure if they were ready for this exam, but now he was confident. He didn't know exactly how strong the other teams would be but was confident in Sayuri and Kota to pull through.

Also, Kota with Shinji's and Yamato's help had been able to get through the hurdle and understood that killing was just part of his job. If the choice came whether to kill someone for the safety of his teammates, Shinji was certain that Kota wouldn't hesitate.

All three of them casually walked towards the exam building where the first part of the Chunin Exam would take place. Shinji noticed that there were many people waiting around the place, some were laying in the yard around the building, feeling the soft green grass, and relaxing. Amongst them, some had bruises too, showing that they had been in fights.

"Tch, who the hell are those guys blocking the room to Room 301?"

"I don't know but they're strong as hell. Talking about weeding out the weak."

'This is interesting.' Shinji thought, glancing toward Sayuri as she had the better hearing. She got the message and nodded, but decided not to reveal what she heard right now. Since they had so many potential enemies around them, revealing their abilities like this wasn't good as they didn't know who was listening in on them either. It would be naive to assume no one could read lips, had good hearing, or x-ray vision in this exam.

Shinji observed everything around him, any sign of danger, or strong person. Every single detail that might seem useful in the future was stored in his mind. Small details sometimes change the flow of battle.

Being the always cautious person he was, Shinji had prepared a lot for the exam. Though to the naked eye he might seem like everyone else, maybe the sword on his back or the bandages around his arms making him somewhat different from most other Genin gathered here. But… Well, he was more than ready for this.

Walking in the building, on the second floor, he noticed that a crowd of people had gathered towards room 301. Which was clearly on the second floor, and was room 201 instead, though that had been changed through a Genjutsu. In the application, it was stated that they had to go to the 3rd floor.

Even Kota seemed to notice that, whispering. "Let's move past these clowns."

It was clear that Kota didn't think much of these people that were tricked by such a simple thing. A couple of young guys wear weeding out the weak, stopping them from entering the room. If Shinji was a betting man, he would go all-in with those two 'young' guys being Chunin. Especially since they eerily resemble the gate guards he met when going out for the C Rank Mission.

Shinji was of similar thoughts to Kota, he wasn't going to waste time here. But suddenly he stopped at the sight of a familiar green jumpsuit.

'Guy -sensei?'

That was the first thought that came to Shinji's mind, but such an assumption was dismissed when he saw that it was just a young Genin. He looked like a mini-Guy and got hit by one of the Chunin. He couldn't even dodge... no, more like the Guy-like genin didn't even try to dodge.

'He must be Lee, and I am almost 100% sure that there is no way Guy's protege would get beat up like this. Even a Chunin probably won't be able to beat him. Guy is a monster in Taijutsu, possibly the best currently living Taijutsu master and an amazing teacher. His look-alike student isn't someone I will underestimate.'

Shinji respected Guy, even though he had trained with the man for less than a month. His Taijutsu had grown to levels incomprehensible from before. So Shinji respected Guy quite a lot, someone who only knew Taijutsu, to become such a monstrously strong ninja. It was nothing short of a miracle born due to hard work.

That was why Shinji wasn't convinced at all when he saw Lee getting hit. Whether the 'genin' standing in front of the door were Chunin, it didn't matter.

"Since we have some time until the exam starts, we should observe and see what our fellow Genins can do," Shinji whispered to his teammates. There were some people he planned to keep an eye on, and Lee was one of them. The main one really, as Shinji somewhat knew Guy had some secret technique he only taught Lee.

'Exploding Youth.' That was the description Guy had given, but Shinji knew that anything involved with Youth and Guy would lead to a dangerous move. "But Lee... with how he looks, it's really hard for most people to not underestimate him."

"Here comes the Uchiha," Kota nudged Shinji and pointed towards Sasuke, someone they hadn't seen in a while.

Sayuri narrows her eyes at Sasuke. "He is weak," she concludes, glancing back at Shinji. "He feels weaker than you."

"You should know better than anyone, chakra doesn't necessarily equate to strength," Shinji reasoned, though even he could tell by the way Sasuke moves that he was physically weaker too.

'Strange... in the Academy, it felt like the gap between me and him was insurmountable. An Uchiha, the name alone made it clear that for someone like me it was impossible to catch up.' Shinji thought, wondering how much he had changed in such a considerably short time.

Sayuri of course took this moment to tease him. "You look like a fangirl~"

Shinji though didn't hear her words as his gaze was as intense as ever while staring at Sasuke. He didn't know if what he was reading was right, or maybe the last Uchiha in Konoha knew how to hide his power.

Seeing that he was so concentrated, Sayuri's smirk disappeared and she approached, her lips next to his ear, and whispered. "If you want to test yourself against the Uchiha, I can arrange it for you."

"No," Shinji shook his head, a calm look adorning his face. "We can't allow ourselves to get any kind of injury during this time. Even wasting Chakra wouldn't be smart."

Still, while he didn't plan on getting involved in a physical fight, that didn't mean that he wouldn't observe and see what the likes of Lee and Sasuke were capable of.

"We are just thinning those who fail. What's wrong with that?" Remarked one of the suspected Chunin.

"I agree, but, you will let me pass through," Sasuke intervened, with his hands in his pockets and a small smirk on his face. "And also remove this surrounding created by Genjutsu."

When he heard those words, Shinji wondered whether Sasuke was stupid, arrogant, or maybe both. Was it a part of a plan? But from what Shinji saw, Sasuke seemed to be arrogant and hadn't changed too much from the Academy days. Which was a little disappointing.

Shinji wondered if this was maybe because Sasuke never had a challenge. Someone who would pass him as soon as he stopped working hard. For example, Shinji knew that people with talent would destroy him as soon as he stopped working hard. But he didn't see that as a negative as it constantly pushed him to be better and work harder.

"I'm going to the third floor," Sasuke stated and started walking off. Sakura and Naruto followed after him. The blonde hyperactive ninja looked on with jealousy as he muttered something about Sasuke always acting cool.

"Oh~ looks like we have a bonafide badass," said one of the disguised Chunin in a mocking voice.

Fwish!

One of them, the one with a bandage over his nose and spiky hair moved quickly. But Sasuke was able to react and was about to counter. Within an instant, Lee was between both of them, catching their attacks without difficulty.

Even Shinji was impressed by his speed. Lee was faster than him, which was expected as he had trained with Guy for much longer. But Shinji glanced at Lee's legs.

"So fast, even with weights," while he didn't know the exact amount of the weights Lee was wearing, Shinji was somewhat sure that he probably was wearing some heavyweights. He had heard Guy mention them in a conversation once.

Still, it wasn't just strength and speed that were required to move those weights, but monstrous stamina too. Shinji knew that even though he was relatively fast, keeping up that speed took a huge effort in his stamina. Lee on the other hand was unlikely to have a problem like that, as he had trained for a year with Guy.

'I am still weak, if we fought right now in Taijutsu, Lee would destroy me without much difficulty. Or, maybe I would be able to hold him back a little while until I started getting tired.'

"What happened to the plan?" The white-eyed teammate of Lee came forward. Shinji could tell that he was a Hyuga. "You're the one who said that we shouldn't draw attention to ourselves."

After that, Lee walked towards Sakura and expressed his love for her. Saying that he would protect her until his death. Which Shinji found weird, as they had just met. But decided to ignore that, as he was more interested in their fighting capabilities. Especially Neji, as he had the Byakugan, but Shinji didn't know a lot about those eyes, or what they did. Be only had heard in some lectures that the Hyuga Clan was considered one of the strongest in Konoha and was a rival to the Uchiha before the massacre.

"What's your name?" Suddenly, Naji glanced at Sasuke. His shallow white eyes somehow showed a sign of amusement in them.

"Ah, man, everyone always wants to only know Sasuke's name," Naruto complains.

Shinji on the other hand was observing Lee closely as this happened.

'He has youth in his eyes. Spending so much time with Guy, I can somewhat guess what will happen now. With overflowing youth, he is going to challenge Sasuke. Wait... when did I start referring to certain things as 'youth'?. Jeez, due to spending so much time with him, I have learned some bad habits.'

...

While Shinji contemplated his existence, and whether Youth was a real tangible energy or if it could be counted. He stood by the sidelines while Sakura took Sasuke and Naruto away, with Lee following them.

Shinji glanced toward Sayuri. "We should follow them."

As a team, they had to take measures and come to an agreement together. While Shinji was still the de facto leader, it didn't mean that he had to act like he was the only opinion that mattered in the team.

"Yes," Sayuri agreed with him. "Sasuke is expected to be good. But Lee... that guy isn't talented in either Genjutsu or Ninjutsu. No, not just untalented at them, he literally can't use either."

"Hmm, but he still seems strong," Kota added. "He isn't like the normal ninja. We have to see how he fights, or that guy... Lee could end up being a tricky opponent to deal with."

Since they were all in agreement, Team 13 followed their fellow Genins, to see what they were going up against. Get a read on how strong their competitors were. There was still some time until the Chunin Exam started.

While Lee followed Sasuke and his team, Shinji and his team were following Lee. They all ended up in a hallway, with Lee above Team Seven, looking down at them from atop the balcony. "Hey, the guy with the dark eyes."

"What is it?" Sasuke glanced up, coolly.

"Fight me, will you..." it wasn't a request. Everyone could tell that.

Fwish!

Lee jumped up, and within an instant landed in front of them. But as he did so, he looked up, and his eyes met with Shinji's. "You're someone I want to fight too."

Sasuke and the rest of his team looked up in surprise, seeing Shinji, Sayuri, and Kota standing on the ceiling upside down. They had used the shadows to hide their bodies, but Lee had noticed them.

"Sorry for the interruption," Shinji smirked. "I and my teammates just wanted to see some entertainment. Not every day you get to see an Uchiha fight."

"Guy -sensei speaks highly of you," Lee nodded, looking back towards Sasuke. "My name is Rock Lee. So you're up for a challenge, Sasuke Uchiha?"

"Heh, you know of the Uchiha and yet you still want to fight me, bushy brows" he exclaimed mockingly.

'What? Why's Sasuke acting arrogant, didn't he see Lee stop his kick so easily? That bushy brow is likely a small beast in a human's body.'

Shinji was confused, while he could understand Sasuke's confidence during the academy, as he was the best back then by a long shot. But that was no longer the case.

"Hey!" Naruto suddenly yelled out, bringing everyone's attention towards him. "Sasuke this, Sasuke that. It pisses me off!" He peered at Lee angrily. "This will be over in five minutes."

He charged at Lee, and the look on Naruto's face was angry as he pulled his fist back.

Shinji... observed with disappointment. 'Slow, Naruto is very slow. That stance is the Basic Academy Style, even that, is very unpolished. Didn't he learn anything as a Genin?'

Then Lee, as if to prove him right, casually pushed Naruto's punch aside, kicking the legs under him and making the whiskered boy's body spin out of control and face slam into a wall.

"You guys cannot defeat me," Lee declared. "Right now, I am the strongest Genin in Konoha."

Sasuke smirked. "Sounds fun, I will fight you."

"Don't," Sakura intervened. "Sasuke, we only have thirty minutes to submit our applications."

Sasuke's confidence didn't falter. "Don't worry, I will take care of this in five minutes."

He charged towards Lee, and once again, Shinji was left disappointed, as Sasuke was able to dodge the first kick. The second one landed to the side of his face.

Baam!!

Slamming Sasuke right into the wall. Blood dripped down from the Uchiha's mouth as his eyes were shadowed by his hair for a split second, but as he looked up, his red eyes became apparent. Two tomoe slowly swirling around his pupil.

'So that's the Sharingan. It looks intimidating.'

Shinji had high expectations for Sasuke Uchiha, the guy that he had been unable to defeat ever in the academy, no one ever had even come close to beating him back then. But the Sharingan was a mighty Kekkei Genkai with the ability to copy Ninjutsu, Genjutsu, and even Taijutsu.

But once again, Shinji was left to be disappointed as Lee was able to easily slip past Sasuke's guard and kick him in the chin. This sent the Uchiha high in the air and disoriented him, as his brain rattled around his skull.

Lee jumped up too, standing behind Sasuke, just like a shadow. Bandages started unraveling and Shinji immediately recognized the technique. Having seen something similar demonstrated by Guy.

'Shit! Is Lee planning to kill Sasuke?! If I don't intervene right now, he will be defenselessly slammed into the ground and his brains will splatter.'

Shinji was about to intervene, seeing that the hit on the chin had immobilized Sasuke. But should he interview at all? This will cause Sasuke's team to be dismissed from the exams, and Lee might be disqualified, which would cause almost all of the strong people in the Chunin exams till now, to thaw out.

But at the same time, he didn't know what kind of monsters this Chunin Exam held. Rather than figuring it out on his own, having some talented Uchiha, or someone like Lee test the waters first would be better.

_____

[Choose]

A - Intervene. Shinji needs some mules to take the burnt of any monstrous Genin.

B - Let it happen. Shinji thinks there is a high chance of Sasuke dying if Lee uses the secret technique. Even at best, Sasuke will probably end up in a coma.

_____

ANNOUNCMENT: For every 100 Power Stones, Shinji gets to re-roll a bad dice roll which usually determines luck.

(If you want more detail, check Discord Announcements)

https://discord.gg/wbwRTqd7jr

Chapter 20: Chapter 20: Springtime of Youth 2

A - Intervene. Shinji needs some mules to take the burnt of any monstrous Genin.

_____

Chapter 20: Springtime of Youth

***

-Yamato POV-

Within the podium where Lee and Sasuke were fighting, I and a couple of my fellow Jonins were stealthily hiding, observing our students from one of the corners.

When Guy saw that Lee was about to use the primary lotus, he frowned, muttering. "That silly boy. Letting his youth get the better of him. But then again, I can understand where he is coming from."

It was unclear whether Guy was disappointed or encouraging Lee. Maybe both? But now it has become clear that this should be stopped before any of our students get hurt before the exam.

But before Guy could intervene, Shinji had jumped between them, with incredible strength and speed, surprising even Lee, and catching him off guard.

"C'mon now, we can't go around being so harsh to fellow Konoha Genin," Shinji smiled nonchalantly. Whether it was easy for him, or it was to unnerve his opponent, I didn't know for sure.

Lee frowned and was about to kick him out of the way, but while midair the maneuverability was limited and Shinji threw some shuriken, which grabbed into Lee's bandages and pinned them to a wall, tugging Lee away and making him lose balance.

But Shinji wasn't finished as he grabbed Lee by his shirt and threw him towards the wall like a ragdoll before the kick could land on him. He also made sure to deliver his own kick, to add to the momentum of pushing him away.

Baam!

Lee smashed into the wall with surprising force, cracking the hard concrete behind him, as a small drop of blood dripped down his lip. The young Genin had a frown on his round eyes. But Shinji didn't pay attention to him any longer, and instead grabbed Sasuke by the back of his shirt, like a cat, and made a water clone to use as a foothold to jump down faster than gravity could take hold.

Good, being mid-air if Lee had decided to attack again would be a bad idea. The clone was destroyed due to being used as a foothold, and Shinji had kicked off it hard enough to land on the ground faster, turning the water clone into a small drizzle of water.

Sasuke had been stunned as his body still shook due to the aftershock he took from the initial kick Lee landed on his chin. I couldn't blame the young boy for being physically unable to move, I can only imagine the power behind that kick. Lee had probably trained that same kick hundreds of thousands of times, Sasuke stood no chance.

"Hey, pinky," Shinji called over Sakura, the casual and gentle smile never leaving his face. "Come and take care of your teammate," he glanced at Sasuke for a second. "Also be careful when picking your fights next time, because this is the Chunin Exam and there are many people stronger than me."

Well, he might not know that, but I doubt there are many people stronger than you. Shinji had just shown just how easily he handled Lee, even I am surprised he did so easily while showing very little about himself. As expected of him. Still, Shinji had the habit of underestimating his abilities sometimes. This is likely due to a life of mediocrity, where he wasn't special in any way.

"Just from seeing the technique once, he figured out a way to cancel the primary lotus. Using a projectile to tug away the bandages that are used to wrap around the opponent," Guy didn't seem mad at his technique being seen through so easily, instead, he had a wide smile, which showed his glistening teeth. "Lee will have a fine rival."

Of course, Shinji is my amazing student. One day he will surpass Tobirama Senju, who took 20 S Rank Ninja to kill. But my student will overcome that and become stronger.

I felt a burst of pride sprout through my heart and had to try my best to control a giggle escape from me. Yes, he will one day make the whole world know his name, and who he is. That's my belief in Shinji, and that's something I believe in so much, I'm willing to put my life on the line for it.

"That guy is something else," even Kakashi, who was reading his Icha Icha Book while his student was getting beaten, commented on Shinji. Pulling up his headband, the Sharingan was in full view. "He has grown again from the last time I saw him."

YES! I know! Your students are all trash in front of him! Even Sasuke Uchiha, who is said to be talented, seemed like a weak academy student in front of Shinji!

Okay, maybe I should tone it down and make sure Kakashi doesn't notice. But Shinji was humble enough for both of us. Turning towards my colleague, I saw Kakashi's lone Sharingan staring right at me. Did he see through my calm demeanor?

"Your heart rate is increasing," was all Kakashi said, before turning back toward Shinji. Oh right, I doubt Lee will take this lying down. Tch, I will need to make sure that Shinji gets out of this in a condition that doesn't ruin his chances during the Chunin Exam, if Guy and Kakashi have anything to say about it, then I don't care.

Lee landed on the ground and peered at Shinji, looking a little annoyed. "Why did you interfere?"

"Because you were going to use a dangerous move. Could have killed him, the last Uchiha. This wasn't done just to save him, but you too. After all, as a Konoha ninja, killing Sasuke Uchiha in such a place, you would likely be met with extreme punishment for your deeds." Shinji explained his reasoning in detail and made sure to not leave anything behind.

Lee's frown slowly turned into a smile and gave Shinji a thumbs up. "I see, then I am thankful for your worry! But I wasn't going to kill a comrade either and would have held back."

"Oh, I didn't know that. From the way I saw it, you could have taken him out without using such a dangerous technique," Shinji stated his observations, which were true as it was clear Lee was leaps and bounds above Sasuke during the whole fight.

I can't help but smile at Shinji showing his compassionate side, which he didn't usually do unless it involved his teammates. He made friends with everyone. Even that hard-headed Eagle, which is known to be a very unfriendly Anbu, only had praises for him.

Still, how will Shinji handle this? From the way, he went, and physically interfered, making sure to stay outside of the view of Sasuke's Sharingan, it seems like he didn't want his moves to be copied. Nor reveal too much of what he was capable of.

As expected, Shinji was cautious, so this wasn't a surprise. But how will he deal with this now? Fight Lee and have Sasuke copy his moves? Or maybe try and use water-style jutsu? After all, Sasuke likely had Fire Affinity like most Uchiha, and using water-style jutsu with a Fire Affinity wasn't a good idea as it wastes too much chakra. Maybe knock Sasuke out? But that would earn the ire of the person he saved.

C'mon now Shinji, this is your challenge. How will you handle it? Will you end up using Jutsu, or truly not show anything and intentionally lose, or retreat? Impress everyone here like you usually impress me. Show everyone that you aren't predictable!

As if hearing my thoughts, Shinji crouched down, very low, and Lee ran towards him at incredible speed that had no place belonging to a Genin. Hell, even a Chunin normally wouldn't be that fast.

His speed was something incredible, and he could likely keep it up for long amounts of time too as he had the stamina.

But Shinji did something unexpected and jumped up. The smile on his face was plastered like always, and it undoubtedly unnerved his opponents by how casually he acted, even if the situation was dire.

But why did he jump mid-air, where he wouldn't be able to move away from an attack? Did he panic and make a mistake? But I thought that by now he wouldn't let his nerves get to him, but again, he is just a recently graduated Genin. Or maybe this is part of some bigger plan.

Lee gave chase, jumping up and within an instant being in front of Shinji. Showing that he was still faster than him, but contrary to his situation Shinji wasn't panicky, and just calmly stared at his opponent. "Bad move," he muttered. "You should remember one crucial detail about Genin, we are..."

At first, Lee was confused about what he meant by that. But the confusion didn't last long, as he got his answer.

"...always a three-man team," this time the voice came from above, finishing Shinji's sentence.

Kota had pulled out his sword, and Sayuri's eyes widened to an unnatural degree with an eerie atmosphere around her, as a strange chakra formed around. Lee winced, having forgotten about Shinji's teammates for a split second.

Well, I don't blame him, I had forgotten too. Shinji wasn't here to fight fairly, but to get this over with while differing minimal or no injury or waste chakra.

Kota Kicked off the ceiling he was standing upside-down on, gravity helping him speed up, and he was in front of Lee within a split second. His sword swing was like formless water. Showing that even without Shinji directly saying anything, they made sure to not reveal their moves or anything.

Clang!

Lee was barely able to take out a kunai to stop the sword, but he was still pushed back from the surprise attack. At the same time, Sayuri landed in front of Sasuke, obscuring his view of the battle. It seemed like she had also understood what needed to be done for Kota and Shinji to fight a little more freely.

"I think you should go to the Chunin Application Room, or you will be late," the sweet smile on Sayuri's face made it seem like this was a choice she was giving them but the eerie aura around her said something different. It made Sakura pale and nod rapidly, poor girl, she probably hadn't even heard what Sayuri said and just agreed due to fear.

I couldn't help the smile on my face that slowly widened. Such perfect teamwork, not even a word had been exchanged between them, yet they all knew what to do.

For a split second, even I had forgotten that both Sayuri and Kota are talented ninjas too. They usually just get overshadowed by Shinji. But both of them were amazing in their own right.

Since Sayuri had blocked Sasuke's view, Shinji, without even needing to look, seemed to have understood what the plan was and what she had done. Kota, using his sword as a baseball bat, and Shinji's foothold, shot teammate toward Lee at breakneck speeds as the air seemed to scream as he shot through it.

Lee tried to react, but this time it was too late, he had been on guard against Sayuri, and during that split second to see what she was doing, Shinji's knee had sunk into his stomach. Grabbing into his shoulders, for extra damage too. He could feel Lee's sturdy ribs brush against his knee.

But even with the pain of being hit, Lee grabbed his opponent's leg. Taking a breath, it seemed like a burning blaze had been lit up inside his eyes.

<First Gate: Gate of Opening… OPEN!>

Shinji's eyes widened, and I was surprised too as Lee's strength seemed to have increased 5x as he clenched down, Lee's fingers clenching around his leg so tight that it was painful. And then he was thrown to the side like a rag doll.

Fwosh!

But mid-air Shinji was able to maneuver himself and land on his feet side-ways into the wall, using chakra to stick to it.

Baam!!

Still, his place of landing cracked all around him like a spider web. "What was that?" muttered Shinji, strangely he didn't seem to be afraid at all. Instead, the look in his eyes only showed curiosity.

That was the Eight Gates… one of the most dangerous Jutsu out there, both to the opponent and the user.

At the same time, Kakashi whispered, his Sharingan glancing at Sayuri. "Yamato, that female student of yours. Her Chakra Network is-"

"Yes, I know."

Sayuri's chakra network was a little… strange for her age. But that isn't all there is to it, her learning of Genjutsu was quite fast. Of course, whether it was really "learning" or maybe just using what she already knew was something debatable. My specialty might not be torture and interrogation, but I knew when to spot something obvious.

She had her secrets, which I didn't pry into. Maybe she was part of some clan, with a Kekkei Genkai, but just like my Wood Style, I am willing to keep this secret of hers. Though if she had a Kekkei Genkai, or it was just some mutation that weakened her Chakra, it was unknown.

My team has shown talent, and I will do everything in my power to make them shine brightly. Whether it's Shinji with his unbreakable will and ambition, or Kota with his dream of becoming an S Rank.

Even Sayuri, wanting to live her life freely, without the attention of the world on her, and just spend time with Shinji. I will support them all. It's my duty as their Jonin teacher, mentor, and as someone who cared about those little talented misfits.

"Guy, shouldn't you stop this?" Said Kakashi suddenly, bringing me out of my thoughts.

"Not yet," Guy smiled widely. "I want both Lee and Shinji to see that there is a wide world out there. Also, Lee will have to be punished for using the Gates."

I somewhat understood his reasons too. In the Forest of Death we won't be able to protect them, so at least this way they'll get an understanding that enemies can be very dangerous.

"For now their flames of Youth must burst through!" Guy's yell was thankfully nullified by a quick noise-canceling Jutsu from Kakashi.

***

Shinji was surprised, he had expected Lee to have some secret technique. But he hadn't expected him to use it right now.

'Damn it, why is he taking this so seriously? The exam hasn't started yet and I was almost injured. Still, that technique should also have some major drawbacks. Increasing the body's power so much is unnatural. So maybe waiting this out and just dodging might be the best until those drawbacks sink in.'

But at the same time, the last thing he wanted was a drawn-out fight. His stamina couldn't keep up, but the same was for Lee too. How long could this technique last? Something increasing its user's strength so drastically most likely had very heavy drawbacks. But Shinji didn't know the specifics of it, maybe it would take days for the major drawbacks to show, and he still had an exam to take in about 25 minutes.

"Oy, oy, oy. Lee, do you want to end the Chunin Exam before it even starts," he could think of many ways to offset the sudden boost Lee got in his physical might. But Shinji was reluctant to do so, and found it very regretful, having to waste Chakra before the exam even began for real.

"Sorry! But as my rival, I have to give it my all or it will be disrespectful to the effort you have put in."

'No, please disrespect me. I wouldn't mind. That way I wouldn't have to even fight here at all.'

Shinji felt like crying, as the sight of Lee charging towards him was the same as seeing every one of his plans shatter like glass. Still, there wasn't anything he could do about it and didn't dwell on the situation for longer than a second. He couldn't afford to do so, even if he wanted to.

Lee was fast, still, monstrously fast, but still not fast enough to stop Shinji from pulling out a scroll.

Poof

A scroll as big as his body came out of that smaller one. Now it was time for him to use his ultimate technique and take care of Lee. Something that Shinji has prepared as his ultimate strategy.

But Lee himself wasn't a slouch and could tell that he would be at a disadvantage soon. "As expected of my rival. I can't go easy on you."

'Go easy on me! I don't fucking mind, nor would I be offended if you did. Also, when did I become your rival?!'

"Let us show each other our overflowing YOUTH!" Lee yelled out, as the flame in his eyes seemed to burn ten times brighter.

<2nd Gate: Gate of Healing, OPE->

'Shit!'

Shinji bit his finger, drawing some blood.

[Summon-]

Fwish!

Baam!

Both were interrupted as Yamato appeared and grabbed Shinji's hand, stopping him from using that technique.

"Lee!! You fool!!" Guy on the other hand had used a more drastic method of stopping his student. By kicking him in the face, having him harshly land on the ground. "How dare you use a technique I forbid you to use! Also, are you trying to ruin your chances and Shinji's by tiring yourself out before the exam! Think! You fool!!!"

Youthful tears came out of Guy's eyes, as he went and hugged the downed Lee. "Letting your YOUTH cloud your thoughts and youthfully having you find an eternal rival."

Shinji decided to dodge that scene by scurrying to the sidelines with Yamato. Kakashi was there too and seemed to be consoling Sasuke about something. The Uchiha had been done in by only one attack. Sayuri, who was obscuring his view, saw that the battle was over and scurried toward Shinji with a happy smile on her face. "You were so cool back there~"

At the same time, Yamato handed Shinji a small pouch. "Since Guy has taught Lee that technique. You'll need a little help too."

Opening the pouch, Shinji winced at the sour smell. But he caught sight of something that surprised him inside.

'Soldier Pills!'

He was surprised by the contents. This wasn't something someone could get their hands on easily, especially a while pouch of them. There were at least 30 of them there.

Soldier Pills are special pills that nourish the body and can replenish one's chakra. It is made up of powerful stimulants and nutrients that are near-instantly absorbed into the intaker's body and said to allow the user to keep fighting for three days and three nights without rest. At the end of the three days effect, the user is brought to the point of complete and utter exhaustion.

A dangerous substance with drastic side effects, but could help someone massively in a desperate situation.

"Woah! Yamato -sensei is giving us drugs?" Kota exclaimed in surprise, which earned him a bashing atop his head. "Ow! Sorry, sorry, I was just joking around."

While walking away, as soon as Yamato noticed that no one was around he started speaking in a low voice where only his students could hear him. "Be careful in this exam. If you need to take the Soldier Pills, make sure to take them when you're at least on the brink of chakra exhaustion. That way you can gain the most out of the regenerating chakra. Also, against the Sharingan, the Hidden Mist technique is quite effective. Also, Shinji, what Lee used is the Eight Gates technique, and what you saw just now was barely the tip of the iceberg. So be careful."

After saying that, Yamato walked off nonchalantly as if he hadn't shown very clear favoritism towards his students. While technically he didn't break any rules, what he did would be considered to the brink of breaking rules. Especially giving information on how to combat against the Sharingan.

"You know, unlike what most people would assume from his usual demeanor, Yamato -sensei can be surprisingly corrupt," Sayuri commented, with a small smile on her face.

When corruption was done to impede you, then you would be hateful. But what if that same corruption and favoritism were done to help you? Well, that changed the situation, also the Chunin Exams were a matter of life and death. Yamato simply didn't want to see his students die.

Shinji also learned something new during this battle. 'Lee is going to be one of the biggest obstacles against me during this exam. Maybe the biggest.'

But on top of all that, what had caught Shinji's eye was another thing. The Eight Gates technique. Of course, he made sure to not have his greed show outwardly and didn't know the exact side effects of the technique. But Shinji wanted to learn the technique, it wasn't a matter of whether it was useful or not either, but as a Jutsu enthusiast, a technique like that was fascinating. He had never seen something like it before, maybe the Body Flicker, but that worked under completely different rules.

...

After dividing the soldier pills amongst themselves, with ten each, Team 13 went towards room 301 and entered. Shinji was glad to not have arrived at the same time as Lee, as he didn't want to meet his new rival for a long while.

But when he entered the room, it was filled with Ninja. At the doorway, there were also nine of his classmates. With a lanky, white-haired man that seemed some years older than them, and with round glasses explaining to Naruto and the others about the Chunin Exams.

Sayuri gave a silent signal to be careful against the white-haired man and Shinji understood that he wasn't as simple as he seemed. Though that seemed already quite obvious. As he reminds me of Mizuki, the slimy bastard. But still, as the man, Kabuto, introduced himself he offered everyone some free info on an individual of their choice.

"Rock Lee, Gaara of the Sand, and Shinji," Sasuke said, without missing a beat.

"Oh? You already know their names? That makes it too easy," Kabuto chuckled good-naturedly. Then he started with Lee, but Shinji somewhat knew already that Lee was good at Taijutsu, because that was all that the info card said. The Mission record wasn't that important.

With Gaara, Shinji found another person he should keep an eye on. A very dangerous person who even went into a B Rank mission and came out of it uninjured.

Shinji immediately assumed that he was either very good at the replacement jutsu or maybe had some defensive jutsu that hardened his skin. Still, he made sure to keep an eye out for that.

Then, your card was about to be read. "Oh, this is an interesting one," said Kabuto, a smile slowly coming to his face as he glanced toward Shinji. No, Shinji felt like he was glancing at the one next to him, Sayuri. "Information on him is very scarce. Especially due to a certain someone."

_____

[CHOOSE ONE, and white it down in the comments below:]

A - "Stop," Shinji decides to verbally stop him. Make it as threatening as possible in case he still tried to reveal it. Shinji didn't know what the man was thinking, or how strong he was. But if he was playing a persona, then he had to keep to that person and back off.

B - Throw a kunai at the card. Shinji didn't want anyone to read it, and this will destroy the card. This might annoy Kabuto. Let's see just how much he can control his emotions, or maybe show an opening.

C - Cast a Genjutsu on the card. Make it show something else.

D - Let it happen. It doesn't matter anyway, as Shinji doubted anyone was able to reveal anything people didn't know. From what he saw from Lee's Card, only what he was good at was revealed, and nothing about the Eight Gates.

_____

A/N: For every 100 Power Stones, Shinji gets a re-roll in a bad dice roll. (which determine luck-related events).

Join discord where I post the dice rolls of the chapter and their effects. And discuss with other readers about plans for Shinji:

https://discord.gg/wbwRTqd7jr

Chapter 21: Chapter 21 - Problematic People 1

D - Let it happen. It doesn't matter anyway, as Shinji doubted anyone was able to reveal anything people didn't know. From what he saw from Lee's Card, only what he was good at was revealed, and nothing about the Eight Gates. (New Perk!)

_____

Chapter 21 - Problematic People

Shinji decided to not intervene and see how this would play out; he too was curious to see how much information Kabuto had on him. Knowing how much a potential enemy knew of him could be useful later on. As long as core techniques weren't revealed, then Shinji saw no reason to not let the guy with the spy-like abilities show just how good he was at his job.

Also by Sayuri's reaction Shinji could somewhat guess that she and Kabuto knew of each other. Maybe the same spy organization? Well, he already knew that she must be some kind of spy, and Kabuto likely is one too. While Shinji didn't pry too much into her secrets, he wasn't naive and already somewhat had a grasp on what was going on.

Of course, this was all just suspicion without any definite proof. But he made sure to keep an eye out for the small details which might become useful in the future.

Poof

The card showed itself, as by using chakra information was burned into it.

========

Name: Shinji

Gender: Male

Nin: Very High

Tai: Very High

Gen: High

Tool: Low

Kekkei Genkai: None

Speed: Very High

Strength: High

Stamina: High

IQ: Very High

Teammates:

Yamato (Jonin Teacher)

Kota Harada

Sayuri

Missions:

D Rank: 16

C Rank: 1

B Rank: 0

A Rank: 0

S Rank: 0

=======

"Hmmm, Shinji, out of all the ninjas here, I would say that he is the most well-balanced one," Kabuto commented, a small smirk raising to his face.

At the same time, Shinji felt Sayuri next to him gasp. "H -How did he find out?" She whispered, shocked, her eyes were wide in surprise. "Don't tell me... he took matters into his own hands. But when? His information should have been blocked, I made sure even his hospital records-"

Shinji nudged her. "Careful," that seemed to wake Sayuri up from her mental shock. "You're thinking out loud," he then smiled at his teammate. Even he was a little surprised seeing Sayuri so worked up. "Don't worry about such things too much. The past can't be changed. Concentrate on the present."

That seemed to calm the panicking Sayuri. Looking around, she was glad that no one, other than Shinji, had heard her delirious whispering.

"Sorry about that," she apologized to Shinji. "And thank you for not prying into my secrets."

She had enveloped both of them in a jutsu that stopped the transmission of the sound of their surroundings. It was usually used for stealth missions by Anbu, to not allow the users to make any sound as they move. But with such a high mastery over it just reinforced Shinji's theory that Sayuri is a spy.

"Woah. You must be some super high-ranking spy for you to get a technique like this," Shinji chuckled. He wasn't worried about which village her loyalties lay, but if she could teach him some new Jutsu, then he would be happy either way.

Sayuri sighed. "You would be surprised just how lacking in control when spreading out certain techniques a certain someone is. He doesn't care about the potential harm they might cause. Also at least act surprised, or like you didn't know."

"Hmm, is that so..." Shinji smiled at her and nodded, ignoring her latter comment. Why act surprised when he already had a theory that was seemingly quite correct the more he saw into it. "Don't worry. I know you won't do something harmful to me."

Shinji wasn't the kind of guy who would trust someone blindly, but with what he had seen until now, the chances of Sayuri working against him were very unlikely. Whether she was a spy or not didn't matter, as spies were human too, able to develop feelings, and she was a good friend. If Sayuri hadn't taught him many things that she shouldn't know already, then Shinji knew that he likely wouldn't have caught onto her real identity.

Maybe she wanted to reveal herself to him? But didn't know how to do it in a good way and just did it through Jutsu? Well, Shinji, again, didn't know that for a fact.

Sayuri clenched her hand at that. "Damn," she looked down. "If you keep saying things like that..."

Whatever she was about to say was interrupted as Kabuto continued explaining. "In the Academy he didn't show any signs of being too special. Though his grades during tests were quite good, even though he didn't seem to try that hard in academic studies and cared more about the jutsu aspect of studying. But under his Jonin teacher's tutelage, Shinji showed genius-like progress. While Sasuke might have been rookie of the year, Shinji can be considered as the strongest of that generation."

'This guy has a lot of information on me. While he might have not said out loud what my elemental nature is, or where my weaknesses might lie... he probably knows.'

Shinji made sure to make a mental note of Kabuto and keep an eye on him but wasn't too worried enough to panic about what he might know. Shinji didn't have any absolute weakness. Whether it was Ninjutsu, Taijutsu, or Genjutsu, he would consider himself moderately competent for his rank in each of the categories.

This guy was very suspicious. But for now, there wasn't anything he could do about Kabuto, instead, Shinji made sure to observe the others and what they thought of

him.

If Kabuto turns out to be as dangerous as Shinji thinks he is, then it would be good to have a trap prepared. One where he would be destroyed, after all, he didn't like leaving people, who seem to be dangerous to someone close to him, to run about freely.

He didn't know the exact situation with Sayuri, but he had a rough guess of what was going on here. But Kabuto... well, a lot of ninjas die every now and then, Sayuri's worry won't last for long.

Shinji wasn't planning on a direct confrontation, but a more stealthy approach to things. He had never done something like this before. But there was a first time for everything.

And of course, this will all be handled cautiously, as so was Shinji's nature of doing things. These were all plans for now, but as soon as the Chunin Exams were over, he planned to have a talk with Sayuri and make sure that her past didn't come to haunt them or put them in danger.

"What?!" Ino screeched. "How would you know that Shinji, who I don't even remember being in our classroom, ends up stronger than Sasuke -kun? Your information sucks, and it's probably untrue."

Shikamaru shrugged. "Actually..." but he stopped himself from saying anything as he noticed the blazing stare Ino sent him, so in the end, finding the situation too troublesome he decided to concede. "Sure, sure, whatever you say."

The Nara Clan heir glanced toward Sasuke and Sakura, which didn't refute the claims of Shinji's strength and by the look on his eyes, the lazy guy seems to have figured something out.

"Hey, hey, don't talk bad about Shinji with me around," Kota intervened before anyone could say anything more. He pulled out his sword, his gaze as sharp as a kunai, ready to cut down anyone who had the guts to bad mouth his friend. "I will slit your throat you stupid bitch."

"What did you say?!" Ino, not knowing fear didn't back down in her confrontation. But as Kota got closer she stepped back, as a fearful gaze came to her eyes as she saw his sword. Immediately, Choji and Shikamaru stood in front of her. Now she seemed to understand that some people were truly dangerous here.

Shinji, seeing that the situation might develop into another fight, put his hand on Kota's shoulder and as his friend glanced at him, he shook his head. "C'mon now. This is enough."

That was enough to convey the message. "Sorry, got too worked up there," Kota sighed, putting his sword back in its sheath. "It's just seeing these people bad mouth you, even after all the hard work... It just leaves a bad taste in my mouth. They have no idea what you have gone through."

The hours Shinji put into training were many. But he didn't consider his hard work that special. It was just what he had to do, to be able and keep up with the others.

Suddenly a heavy murderous intent crashed toward Shinji, like a tidal wave, looking toward the source, it was a red-haired Genin with the word love written on his forehead.

'What a heavy bloodlust, it makes a chill go down my spine. I don't think even the average jonin can develop such killing intent.'

Despite what he thought, Shinji didn't show even an ounce of fear towards Gaara, not even a trace of it, while the bloodlust seemed to increase. Until it suddenly stopped as Shinji looked the source right in the eyes.

'For now, it isn't good to draw too much attention to ourselves. But it seems like many of the favored Genin in this exam have their eyes on me.'

The red-haired guy, the Hyuga, Lee, and that guy with the bandages who is peering at Kabuto with murderous intent seem like the biggest threats in this exam. Plus, Kabuto himself too. For now, these were the ones that Shinji had pointed out in his mind to keep an eye out for.

Also, he noticed that Lee seemed a little tired and out of it, likely due to the backlash from his Eight Gates.

Fwish!

Suddenly, the bandaged guy and his teammates moved through the crowd. Taking note of their headbands, Shinji saw that they had the sound village sign.

If he remembered correctly, he had read in some newspaper that the Sound Village was a relatively new hidden village, they're very mysterious too. It's only due to curiosity and reading the news around the world that Shinji knew such a village even existed. But except for its existence, he didn't know anything else about it.

'Did something happen before I came here?' - He wondered as what seemed to be the leader of the Sound Team punched toward Kabuto. Due to the tense atmosphere, and everyone looking toward them, no one else except him seemed to have noticed the Sound ninja coming.

"Hey!" Naruto suddenly yelled, breaking the silence and tense atmosphere. He turned toward the other ninjas, who were sitting on the desks, and some that were laying down on them. "My name is Naruto Uzumaki, and I won't lose to any of you bastards!!"

His yell seemed to gain everyone's attention, and the anger was palpable.

'How... stupid. Didn't Naruto see how Sasuke and his team got destroyed by just Lee? How could he say something like this now? What a fool seems like he hasn't changed at all from his academy days.'

"Those are some big words," muttered Kiba. "What a show-off."

"What a moron, he just turned everyone here into his enemy," added Shikamaru, moving himself to the back of the crowd.

Sakura was the first to react, getting her teammate in a chokehold and looking towards the other Genin. "S -Sorry, he was just joking."

"Huh? What're you talking about? I was being honest." Naruto, of course, spilled out the truth anyways.

Shinji almost signed but was infinitely glad that none of them were in his team. Also, Sasuke's team seemed to be too chaotic, with Naruto being a loud mouth and his orange clothes, that Shinji thought he would abandon as a Genin. Though he could use transformation to cover that during missions, it still wasn't a good idea to wear such clothes, as transformation couldn't be held forever and sounded like useless work. That could easily be solved by wearing normal clothes.

Especially in an exam like this. To do such a thing, it showed to Shinji that Team 7 had one of the worst dynamics here. If not the worst.

Fwosh!

Finally, the Sound Team arrived, which to Shinji they were moving kind of slow, maybe it was due to fighting Lee not so long ago. The one with the spiky hair, and strange holes in his hands threw two kunai at Kabuto, who dodged by jumping back. The bandaged guy, with the strange device in his hand, punched toward Kabuto. He was able to dodge the attack, by a hair's length.

But something strange happened, as his glasses cracked. "Ah, so it was that kind of attack," he muttered, before falling to his knees and throwing up. *Blugh!*

Shinji's eyes narrowed, peering at the strange device on the bandaged man's arm.

"Heh, get that in your stupid info cards," said the spiky-haired Sound ninja. "The Sound Team is going to become Chunin during this exam."

'That attack. Kabuto dodged it, I saw that. But, there was some secret to that Sound guy's attack... wait... sound. Ah, so that's probably the trick to it. In the future, it seems like in a fight, I will have to keep my distance from those guys during a fight.'

Though Shinji was impressed by the ability, he wasn't impressed by the user. Why show something like that? Just because your little pride got hurt? You're a ninja, not a samurai. That pride had revealed a dangerous ability that even Shinji might have gotten done in by. Though now, that same ability had now become useless against him.

'A battle between ninjas isn't one of just power or jutsu, but also one of information too. There are countless abilities out there, and every jutsu has a weakness. Also... that tool in his arm.'

Shinji didn't know the exact mechanics of the arm, but he wouldn't mind studying such a thing. As it would be especially deadly in close-quarters combat. If he had something like this when he fought Lee previously, he would have easily won.

Sayuri frowned and tugged Shinji's shirt slightly, signaling him that those guys would be troublesome too. Nodding, they all went together and sat down at one of the desks. They had assigned seats different from each other, but Shinji made sure that he knew their positions.

POOOF

In a burst of smoke, a man wearing a black coat, with many chunin wearing light gray, almost white uniforms next to him appeared behind Kabuto, Naruto, Kiba, and the others that had gathered at the entrance.

"Oy, you brats, how about you go to your seats," Ibiki Morino intervened, appearing out of a cloud of smoke. The look on his face was emotionless, but the scars made him somewhat seem angry.

Since the setting places were in the application letters, everyone found their place and Shinji was a little surprised to see that the female member of the Sound Team was the one who sat down next to him. He didn't know if this was a good opportunity or an unnecessary annoyance.

Sneakily reading the name in her application letter, he saw that it was Kin Tsuchi. Turning towards him, she smirked. "Shinji, right? The four-eyes said a lot about you. If I was in your place, I would have cut off that fool's hand."

Shinji smiled politely. "Yes, that was a little unpleasant. Even if I was that strong, which I am not," he added. "Having others know about it is unpleasant."

He decided to use her dislike for Kabuto to his advantage. Words were free, so why not use them? Whether he might have to kill her or not later, it didn't matter in the general gist of things.

"Heh, I knew it, that guy's information sucks," she said confidently. "If..." Kin suddenly stopped just as she was about to say something. Staring at Shinji, her smirk widened a little. "You know, that teammate of yours is quite infamous for being cruel. It's surprising to see her acting like this. I know of her from back in the day, she was merciless. Do you know that she's hiding quite a lot of things from you? Is she really someone who cares about her teammates or is that all just an act?"

By the smirk on her face, Shinji could read the girl in front of him like an open book. She wanted to sow discord between his teammates.

Unlike some ninja today though, he knew when to keep his mouth shut and not say anything that would ruin his chances. Sure, let his competition assume whatever they want, assumptions don't change facts.

So acting out his part Shinji frowned, looking disturbed as he was given a test paper. From the corner of his eye, he saw Kin smirking, as if she had already won.

'Why is there so much arrogance in this Chunin Exam? Sasuke, the Sound Team. Sure it might be just four ninjas amongst over a hundred. But that's still way too much for a Ninja. Arrogance doesn't have a place in our line of work.'

Shinji wondered if his understanding of what it means to be a ninja had been an overstatement. After all, they were still human and had their vanities.

"Okay, now that everyone has their papers, let me explain how this exam will work," Ibiki gathered everyone's attention. "This exam will have ten questions, nine will be on the paper. The last question will be revealed 45 minutes after the start of the exam. Those caught cheating will be disqualified."

His eyes roamed around the classroom, as Chunin took their seats by the side, ready to see if anyone would dare to try and cheat in front of them.

"Also, if one of your teammates is caught, the whole team goes with you," Ibiki smirked cruelly.

It was at that moment that Shinji could tell what was happening. 'That man, he is probably a T&I specialist. He is re-enacting this just to make everyone here nervous.'

Shinji acted as Kin expected him to act, a little nervous, though trying to now show it on the outside. The best time to crush someone is when they think they've already won.

Unlike most Genin here, Shinji was wholeheartedly into the ninja career. Whether it came to lying, tricking, or killing, he didn't mind any of them. He has made sure that when he becomes a ninja, he will always keep the right mentality. Seeing what arrogance had done to someone like Sasuke, chills ran down his spine.

'I must make sure that something like that never happens to me. No matter how strong I become, I must never let arrogance take hold of me.'

With those resolute thoughts, Shinji glanced at his test paper and his frown deepened. The questions in it were hard, something that no Genin... no, not even most Chunin would be able to solve them. So it was clear to him, immediately, that the induction of this exam was encouraging them to cheat in a way that they wouldn't be noticed.

'Information gathering. That's the goal of this exam.'

Though Shinji knew some of the answers to the questions himself. So the difficulty of the test was quite clear since, in the Academy, he was one of the best in theoretical knowledge.

Looking around, Shinji noticed that even Kin seemed nervous. What should he do now? He contemplated that for a second.

_____

[CHOOSE ONE, and white it down in the comments below:]

A - Help your teammates by using Genjutsu. Show them the answers by using Genjutsu to create a test paper with the answers you know in front of them.

B - Look around. Silently observe what abilities the others have. Shinji doesn't want to be caught by surprise by an ability like that of Dosu's.

C - Try to sabotage others, putting them under Genjutsu and much more. Shinji thinks this is the best stage to get rid of people he might not be able to beat in a fight.

D - Disregard everything else and concentrate on your exam.

_____

A/N: I rewrote the chapter from its initial version because I didn't like how it came out. That's why it was posted a little late.

Join discord where I post the dice rolls of the chapter and their effects. And discuss with other readers about plans for Shinji:

————

Chapter 22: Chapter 22 - Paper Exam is Over 1

A - Help your teammates by using Genjutsu. Show them the answers by using Genjutsu to create a test paper with the answers you know in front of them.

————

Chapter 22 - Paper Exam is Over

…

Shinji, seeing that the exam might be a little difficult for Kota, thought up an idea to help his friend. Going through some hand signs, he looked at his teammates and saw them looking right back at him. A wisp of chakra, too small for anyone to notice, flew towards his teammates.

[Demonic Illusion: False Surroundings]

Both Sayuri and Kota's eyes turned dull for a split second, as they entered the Genjutsu. But it didn't take long for them to start writing in their exams papers. Every now and then staring in front of them, as if an exam paper was laid there.

Shinji made sure that none of the instructors noticed him. Even if a Jonin was here, he doubted they would notice a Genjutsu being cast on someone else if the victim didn't exhibit any abnormal behavior.

Suddenly, Shinji got images sent back by Sayuri, using Genjutsu. In front of him, something was written, the first couple of paragraphs were about the test, but the rest was different. He could dispel the Genjutsu easily, but this was meant as a mode of communication.

————

Kabuto is a spy for Orochimaru. Be careful, he should be about as strong as an Elite Jonin. Think of him at around Yamato -sensei's level. But if he does something, he is a medical ninja, I don't know a lot about his fighting style. Though his Chakra amount is quite low, use that how you will in case of a confrontation.

P.S: Good idea with the Genjutsu. Never thought of sending messages like this before.

————

Orochimaru. That name came up again and it sent a chill down Shinji's spine. He didn't want to get involved in whatever was happening behind the scenes. He was a simple Genin, his power was nothing compared to one of Sannin. Whatever interest Orochimaru had on him, it was a bad idea to get involved with someone you had no leverage over, and couldn't even meet on equal grounds.

Just thinking about Orochimaru having an interest in him made Shinji have a heart attack, metaphorically of course. As in reality, he wouldn't let his fear overpower him so easily.

'Why can't I just train in peace and not get involved with some super strong Ninja right off the bat. Also having a jonin-level person taking part in the same exam sucks.'

Still, even though he was complaining internally about his bad luck. Shinji's mind was working at its best capability, trying to somehow offset and plan around a situation in which he might encounter someone that dangerous.

If Kabuto was as strong as Sayuri said, then there isn't a lot Shinji could do against a Jonin in a head-on fight. But a ninja rarely fought head-on, especially against someone stronger than you.

...

Forty-five minutes passed quickly. During most of the exam, Shinji spent it thinking of the possible encounters against the Genin here and how he would go about it. Countless hypothetical situations played in his mind.

With him and Sayuri communicating through Genjutsu, they were easily able to solve the questions in the sheet. So their only priority was Kota, who also easily answered the questions and ended up with a huge smile on his face.

While other Genins were panicking, Shinji and his team were relatively relaxed. Well, Sayuri seemed to have her worries. But he doubted her worries were due to the exam.

...

It didn't take long for students to start dropping like flies as they were caught cheating. Some refuted the Chunin, but after some show of power, they were put back in their places.

There was one of the Sand Genin that went out with the extra Chunin inspector to go to the bathroom.

As the exam came to an end, there were many people panicky looking around, clearly, they hadn't had too much of a success in the exam and were panicking.

Amongst them, was Naruto. Shinji had already expected to not be able to solve a paper exam.

"Okay, that's enough," said Ibiki, his harsh cold voice making many people who weren't sure of their answers feel panic crawl up their hearts. "Now the 10th question will be revealed."

Unlike many of the people here, Shinji was as calm as he could be. If he succeeds then that's good, if he fails, then he is okay with that too. It just meant that he wasn't good enough to be a Chunin yet. He hasn't disillusioned himself to think that during his life there won't be some obstacles. He just has to work harder to overcome them.

"But keep this in mind, if you decide to take this last question and fail. You'll lose your chance to ever become a Chunin," though Ibiki talked calmly. His words brought anxiety within a lot of the Genin. "So, do you dare continue?!"

His gaze sharpened as a pressuring aura came out of him. The pressure increased soundlessly and it made the decision even harder. Many saw their ninja carers flash in front of their eyes, no matter how hard they tried it would never be enough.

'What bullshit. As if he has the authority to decide who becomes a Chunin in other villages.'

Shinji immediately saw through his act.

Ibiki was a Jonin, at best. Or maybe a Special Jonin, one specialized in torture and interrogation. Why would that guy have the authority to have someone from another village become an eternal genin? That didn't make sense. Even if they're allied with Konoha, other villages allowing that would just show that they're under Konoha, no worse than slaves.

Also even within the village, to have a ninja's career fail in just such a simple question. It was illogical in every single way.

'As if someone will believe something like that.' - Shinji almost chuckled. Knowing that you would have to be stupid to fall for something like this. Just thinking about it for a second would make the whole thing fall-

"There's no way that's true!" Kiba stood up in anger. "It's unfair to have a whole ninja's career based on this one decision."

Shinji didn't know whether to laugh or cry at this. He couldn't believe someone fell for it, looking around he noticed that many had fallen for the same scheme too. Even Kota seemed a little nervous, but unlike most others, he wasn't shaking in his boots and didn't seem like he would give up.

"What?!" The blonde-haired girl, from the Hidden Sand Village, panicked and stood up. "I know for a fact that there were people from the previous exam who still took the exam this year too."

'Seems like there's someone with a brain. Blonde hair that is tied up in four bundles, she is from the Hidden Sand Village. I will make note of her too. If I am not mistaken, she's in the same team as the creepy red-haired guy.'

"Heh," Ibiki smirked coldly. "So what? It's just your rotten luck that I am your exam proctor this year. I didn't make the rules last time."

In the end, she had no choice but to sit down worriedly. Shinji on the other hand leaned back on his chair, confident with 99% certainty that this was a false threat and a bluff.

"Anyway, if you want to leave, do so now," the smirk on Ibiki's face widened in an almost sadistic manner.

Unable to handle the pressure, one by one, dozens of students started leaving. Teams only needed one member to fall out and they would go down with them too. So just like that, people left in the dozens.

By how crowded the exam room was now, compared to before, Shinji could tell that around 35-40% of the Genin have been disqualified during the exam, and this was only the first part.

"Don't underestimate me!" Suddenly, a yell from Naruto startled everyone, even Shinji, as it came out of nowhere.

Baam!

The orange-wearing ninja slammed his hand onto the table. "I don't quit and I don't run! You can act tough all you want! You're not gonna scare me off! No way! I don't care if I do get stuck as a Genin for the rest of my life! I'll still be Hokage someday!"

'Oh okay, that's cool and all. But why did you have to announce it to everyone out of nowhere? That startled me.'

Shinji still didn't quite understand why Naruto acted the way he did. After all, he could have just kept quiet and not quit, there was no need to declare it out loud. Nonetheless, actions like this were entertaining. Even some of the observers that are here to check in case anyone cheated during the exam, were bewildered by the sudden declaration.

'No wonder everyone thought of him as a bragging loudmouth. He talks the talk, but can't walk the walk. Still amusing to see other people's reactions to him though.'

Shinji wasn't bothered by Naruto for long. But he did notice that the speech seemed to have encouraged some Genin to stay. Which might work in his favor during the next exam. So that made his mood a little better, as the ones who decided to still stay were a little weak and not ready for the exam yet.

Seeing that quite a lot of people had stayed, Ibiki smirked, calmly stating. "Well then, you've passed the First Phase of the Chunin Exam."

""""""WHAT?!!!!""""""

Many people exclaimed in shock, surprised at the outcome. Ibiki shrugged nonchalantly at their expressions. "The 10th question was whether you were willing to take the question or not. Anyone who is still here has passed."

"So this whole exam was for nothing then? What's the point of answering the other questions if we were going to pass like this?" Inquired the blond-haired girl, catching a glimpse of her paper, since she was seated close by he saw that her name was Temari.

"No, information sometimes can be more valuable than life. We put in a couple of decoy Chunins that knew all the right answers. Your job was to find out who they were and cheat off of them without being found." Ibiki then took off his bandana, showing a horrific sight that left everyone stunned.

Even Shinji was surprised by the degree of scars. Burning, cutting, and even screw holes made in his skull. This man had gone through excruciating torture. While to others this might just prove a point about how important information is and how far some are willing to go to get it.

'That... I must make sure I never end up like that. The only way someone can guarantee that they don't end up that way is by being strong enough to not get captured like this. Because not only I might not be able to survive, but it would be a horrible death.'

BREAK!

Suddenly, another startling event happened, as Shinji almost flinched at the sound of the exam room window breaking. And in came the female version of a loud-mouth ninja, just by the smile on her face one could tell she was trouble. Especially with the draped cloth that she had nailed to the wall behind her.

The clothes she wore were very risque. With only a mesh shirt that left little to the imagination, and a light-brown coat to cover her. "Hey there you rats! My name is Anko, and I will be your new and sexy examiner for the next part."

"Anko... I still haven't finished telling them the exact results of the exam," Ibiki responded, emotionlessly. "Anyway," but he turned back toward the rest of the Genin and nodded. "You've also gained the ability to participate in the second exam. My colleague might have-"

"Yeah, yeah, it was all about courage and all that," Anko interrupted him again, blushing in embarrassment. Ibiki likely was going to make it clear in front of everyone just how lame her entrance was as she was off-time. But Anko was in a hurry to stop that, so she pointed towards the broken window. "Follow me, I will take you to the next part of the exam."

Shinji couldn't help but silently chuckle at her behavior, which even Ibiki seemed entertained by. That made Shinji understand that while to Genin, this exam might seem important and something that will determine the waves of their lives. The examiners weren't that worried about it. Instead, they were playing around a little, it was too dull for them.

"Anyway, if you can't keep up with me. Meet at the Forest of Death, also known as training ground 44."

Fwish!

Everyone followed after Anko, as she jumped out of the broken window. Shinji and his team stood together as they jumped from roof to roof of the

...

After a while, they arrived at the corner of Konoha where the Forest of Death stood, with its giant trees making one feel like an ant while standing there. Shinji remembered that the First Hokage's specialty was Wood Style Jutsu and that maybe he was the one who created the forest of death as it was quite an unnatural place. With just one look, anyone would be able to tell that much. How could a forest like that grow in this place when the village's vegetation was normal.

Anko explained all of what would happen in detail, saying that many ninjas could die here and that they needed to sign a waiver before entering. So neither the examiners nor Konoha are held responsible for their lives.

"Heh, you're just trying to psyche me out! And I won't fall for it!" Declaring Naruto, he then imitated her explanation by ridiculing gestures of Anko.

Fwish!

Suddenly a kunai was thrown at Naruto, cutting his cheek before he could react. Within an instant, Anko was behind him and she licked his blood. "Arrogant fools like you are the first ones to drop dead."

Shinji's eyes widened as he saw a Genin sneak up behind Anko, he had long hair, a bamboo hat, and his tongue elongated, holding onto the kunai she had thrown at Naruto before.

"You dropped your kunai," he offered it back to Anko. Shinji was able to tell that while the man sounded feminine. But the body posture as he stood and walked was likely a man.

Still, none of that mattered as Shinji felt chills go down his spine when he recalled the speed the man had moved at. He couldn't even sense his move, which was strange as Shinji even against a Jonin like Yamato could somewhat sense when he was moving.

'That guy is another one of the dangerous people. It seems like even Sayuri doesn't seem to know who he is. Hidden Grass Village seems like they have their own monstrous Genin too.'

Shinji was on edge, it felt like dangerous people kept appearing from out of nowhere. He swallowed as his eyes turned sharp, his senses fully ready, just in case.

Sayuri on the other hand went and offered Naruto a band-aid. "Here you go," she smiled politely. "Make sure no animals in the forest can smell the blood."

"OOh," Naruto blushed. "Thank you. You aren't so bad after all."

Sayuri only smiled and walked off, but as soon as she turned her back on Naruto, her gaze turned cold and she smirked at me. Once she got close, she whispered. "That band-aid has a small storage seal that releases a certain pollen that my summons can smell."

"You have summons?" He knew about the subject a little but never thought Sayuri could already summon living creatures. "I never knew that."

"It's less impressive than it sounds," he sighed as if disappointed by her summons. "Also I believe I don't have to tell you. But don't mention this to anyone."

"Obviously," summoning wasn't something that just any Genin could know, and one thing is for sure: Yamato didn't teach her summoning. If he had taught her, then Shinji would already know it too. "Also that was a good choice since they're the weakest team here."

Well, there was Shikamaru's team too. But they had Shikamaru and they were all part of Clans, so they likely had some secret techniques that Shinji didn't want to try and figure out in the middle of battle.

..

Each team was given one scroll, Shinji had the Heaven Scroll and made sure to put it in a secure place. Now they needed an Earth Scroll, and they would have to safely go to the middle of the forest to pass the exam.

"START!!" The gates opened and all of the genin entered the Forest Of Death.

Trees became a blur as Shinji and his team dashed away from the entrance, making sure to not leave any traces behind.

"Where should we go now?" Sayuri asked Shinji, both she and Kota were expecting a decision from him as the team leader. Whatever he chose, they both would agree with his decision. They were a close team that didn't see a need to fight against each other for things like these.

A - Go North. Towards the tower, you're bound to meet some teams along the way. Shinji doesn't want to spend a second more than he needs in this forest.

B - Go East. That's where Naruto and his team are. Shinji already knows their strengths and they're easy pickings. In his eyes, they're the easiest team to deal with, and likely the weakest. With how well he knows them, they can even do a stealth approach by transforming as Naruto, or Sakura.

C - Go West. You have a week to complete this part of the exam. Take things slowly, and search for other teams. Learn, adapt, overcome.

————————

Chapter 23: Chapter 23

C - Go West. You have a week to complete this part of the exam. Take things slowly, and search for other teams. Learn, adapt, overcome.

————————

Chapter 23

...

"We're going west," Shinji concluded, he thought of many options. Going to the tower so fast could end up with meeting some monstrously strong guys, as they would likely be the first ones to go there. Going with Sasuke's team, since they were the weakest, many other people are bound to go for them too.

Moving through the trees, Shinji could smell the blood around them. Looking down, he saw many animals had been slaughtered and blood was drenching the ground. "What happened here?"

Suddenly, Sayuri stopped, causing both Shinji and Kota to stop too. She pointed towards where they were going. "There are three people who are being hunted by animals in front of us. It feels like they've stepped into a trap."

Hearing this, Shinji almost wanted to smile but stopped himself as they ran past the trees and finally arrived at where it was happening. He saw some people surrounded by big bears, snakes, and tigers. The animals strangely seemed to work together as they attacked.

"They're under a Genjutsu," Shinji concluded, knowing that animals working together like that were very unlikely. The people who were being attacked were two genin from the land of Grass guessing by their headbands. One of them had slightly spiky brown hair and eyes, with an average face. While the other wore a black bandana.

Even when fighting against normal animals they were at a disadvantage, showing that they were quite weak and already had some injuries amongst them.

"Damn it!" yelled out the brown-haired guy. "Where the hell did that red-haired bitch go?! We're dying over here! If we don't get her healing soon... we're gonna bleed out."

Shinji saw this but didn't pay attention to them anymore and instead looked around, trying to figure out who had attacked them. Since these Grass Genin were so weak, why bother going this far, unless they were sadistic? But there was another, more likely scenario, the ones that had put the animals under Genjutsu were even weaker.

Fwish! Fwish! Fwish!

Still, Shinji and his team heard the sound of projectiles cutting the air and that was all the warning they got as countless kunai rained down from above them. Shinji immediately jumped back, so did Sayuri and Kota. But that was when something strange happened, as from one of the trees.

Paam!

A net gun was shot and Kota was caught in it, stopping his retreat, and Shinji could do nothing but watch as he was mid-air. The bloody sight of Kota being hit by dozens of kunai as he tried to block them from hitting any of his vital organs. He couldn't do anything but fall as he was entrapped in a net.

'Shit! If he falls like that he's going to die!'

As soon as Shinji landed on a tree, sideways, chakra surged towards his feet and within less than a second he jumped towards Kota. He now had twenty or more kunai sticking into his body and he seemed to have gone unconscious.

Clang! *Clang!* *Clang!*

Using a kunai, Shinji deflected the rest of the kunai that was thrown at them, and he noticed the small amount of liquid that was coated in them. It was poison, and the situation had become even more dangerous as a deadly poison was flooding Kota's body.

As they landed on the soft grass, Shinji dropped his friend's body on the ground as a deadly silence enveloped him.

"Sayuri, take care of Kota," after saying that, his eyes turned towards the tree where he had noticed the net shoot from.

Fwish!

Within an instant, Shinji's body turned into a log and he appeared in front of a tree trunk, standing in a thick branch.

Baam!!

He punched towards the tree, and his fist met some resistance towards the tree, and slowly as if a veil was taken off, a body was revealed. A female, brown eyes and hair, around fourteen to fifteen. Her eyes were wide in shock, as Shinji's punch had sunk into her chest and caved in her rib cage, puncturing her lungs, causing them to fill with blood and feel like she was drowning in a hot liquid. Her headband showed that she was from the Hidden Rain Village.

Her body slumped to the ground, she hadn't even been able to react to Shinji's attack, nor had she seen it. Also, he hadn't hesitated for a second and immediately went for the kill. Looking up, he heard some slight movements and by using Substitution to move around, with a split second.

Poof!

He was behind two guys, both were wearing gas masks and looking toward Shinji below them, while the replacement still kept its human form so they thought he was still down there.

"W -What the hell was that?" whispered one of them. "We need to get out of here, that guy is danger-"

Fwish!

He didn't get to finish his words as his head flew off. His other teammate, the only one left alive, could do nothing but stare in horror. He immediately dashed forward to escape, but he could do nothing as he felt Shinji put him under chokehold mid-air, one hand below his chin and the other above his head.

"Antidote," Shinji muttered simply, his voice as cold as an ice storm.

"I -It's in my pocket. Please spare-"

CrAaAacK!

With a bone-chilling sound, the man's neck was twisted in an unnatural manner, like a marionette, Shinji exerted strength through his arms and broke his neck off, making sure that he was dead. After that, while still mid-air, he carefully went through the man's pockets and found many vials of poison and some other liquid that he assumed to be antidotes.

He carefully made sure that the dead guy's body wasn't destroyed in case he had lied about the antidote. He calmly walked toward his friend and handed Sayuri the vial of antidote, she opened it and took a sniff. "This should be an antidote."

Shinji just stood there, looking at Kota's unconscious bleeding body. Even as Sayuri administered the antidote, the bleeding alone was enough to kill him. Even if they rushed right now, the movement from taking him to the tower or outside the Forest of Death would likely kill him.

"Do you know any medical jutsu?" asked Shinji, his calm eyes had turned cold as he peered at his dying teammate.

"No..." Sayuri muttered regretfully. "I never even tried to learn it."

"I see," Shinji's words were calm... No, they now had turned cold too. His mind worked harder than it had ever worked before, trying to figure out something where Kota ends up surviving.

'Even if he survives, many of his nerves are cut. His career as a ninja is over, he will never be able to move the body like he needs to. His swordsmanship was the only tool that he had as a ninja which he was good at.'

As Shinji slowly came to accept the ending, and Kota's possible death. An idea struck him, his eyes sharpened like those of a hawk and he turned around.

Sayuri couldn't even see his hand seals, and only saw multiple water clones morphing out of his body.

He left them behind to keep guard, though he couldn't move too far away from them. But he stood where the animals were attacking the two Grass Ninja. Taking out his sword, though not that good at swordsmanship, with his overwhelming strength, Shinji cut off snakes, bears, tigers, and any other animal around. Decapitating them with one swift move, so fast that not even a drop of blood landed on him.

He then stood in front of the two Genin from the hidden grass. They were injured and winced when they saw him. "I heard you talking before about your teammate and healing. Where are they?"

They shook, Shinji's stair was like that of a giant and cold as a snake's. Both knew that if they didn't speak, he would kill them.

"S -She went that way," pointed one of them.

"If I don't find her, make sure you're ready," Shinji warned and with a swift chop to their necks, knocked them out.

He charged, with speeds that he rarely moved at before. Shinji... wasn't the kind of guy who had a lot of friends. Neither did he care about having many of them. But if there was one person who had his back from the beginning, willing to move together with him, and helps with Kenjutsu. It was Kota, he would feel more insulted when someone spoke badly about Shinji rather than himself.

In short, he was Shinji's best friend.

It didn't take long to find Karin, and when he did, she was being chased by a bear. Of course, not long after the bear was still running, but this time without its head. When its body no longer caught signals, it slumped into the ground.

Karin, breathing heavily, turned around to look at her savior and saw Shinji, not a speck of blood was on his clothes. But his hand and word were covered in blood, which was not his own.

"Can you heal someone?" He asked this time more softly as he didn't want to leave a bad impression on the healer and have her be unwilling to heal Kota.

"Y -Yes," she stuttered, looking at him strangely and then at the ground. "M -My name is Karin. What's your-"

She didn't get to finish her words as Shinji grabbed her in a princess carry and blitzed through trees. Karin could barely see anything as they moved, and not much later she was in front of ten other Shinjis which she could sense were some kind of clones.

Also, there was a bleeding young man on the ground, except for his big body and pale face, which was due to blood loss, there was nothing special about him. "Is he the one I have to heal?"

Shinji nodded and pointed towards him. "If you do this for us, we will help you pass this exam. Even give you our scroll."

Of course, when he said that he didn't mention the scroll of the people he had just killed. Because while the situation was dire, Shinji still held his cool and was thinking ahead. He was intrigued, instead of using medical jutsu, the red-haired girl pulled up her sleeve, showing her arm which was full of bite marks.

'Strange. Why are there so many bite marks?'

But he got his answer as soon as she put her arm forward and had Kota bite down, by using chakra to stimulate his jaw muscles. Karin didn't even flinch at the pin, and instead kept glancing toward Shinji. That made Sayuri narrow her eyes, and open her mouth, about to say something, but she stopped herself.

"Also, your teammates. They're safe, I didn't kill them on account of you." Shinji explained while pointing at her two unconscious teammates, whose bodies were slumped to the ground.

Karin's eyes turned cold at that. "Can I cash in that favor that you owe me?"

"Yes," Shinji nodded, looking in awe as color returned to Kota's skin and all of his injuries were healed. He opened his eyes and stood up, perfectly well.

'What?! That isn't just healing jutsus, they take time, and with all of the blood Kota had lost there is no way that he would be up so soon.'

Even Kota himself seemed surprised, staring at his hands in awe and clenching his fists. "This isn't a dream, right?" he muttered quietly, but Shinji was able to hear him.

"I want you to kill my teammates," Karin suddenly stated, a cold, devilish smile coming toward her face. "I will kill them all. Hidden Grass Village, I will kill them all for what they did to my mother."

Shinji sensed that there were some issues there, but decided to not ask and instead just threw two kunai at breakneck speeds.

Puk! *Puk!*

The sound of skulls being pierced rang out, as the kunai Shinji threw and killed her teammates without any hesitation. Karin then took out an Earth Scroll and handed it over to Shinji. "Here, I don't need this thing anymore."

Since he already had a Heaven Scroll, two like the team he had killed ruthlessly had another heaven scroll. With Karin's Earth Scroll, then he could easily pass this exam.

'I am not staying here for long. This place is dangerous for Kota and even Sayuri. We must move towards the tower!'

But as he turned around, he saw Karin glancing at the ground, with sadness filling her eyes. Remembering how she couldn't even do basic ninja techniques, Shinji wondered if he should help her.

Technically, he had repaid his debts with her, and they were even. But he still felt thankful toward the red-haired girl.

————————

[Choose one of the choices, and white it down in the comments below:]

A - Help Karin get to the tower safely.

B - Don't help Karin

————————

Author Note:

Kota survived due to luck, literally. Due to rolls which decide luck, Karin and her team were close by.

P.S: For every 100 Power Stones, Shinji gets a re-roll in a bad dice roll. (which determines luck-related events).

Chapter 24: Chapter 24 - The Tower

A - Help Karin get to the tower safely.

****

Chapter 24 - The Tower

***

What a Genin knew and could do was only so much.

Shinji could feel the sense of relief spread through his body. He was worried and nervous. Being a leader came with a lot of responsibilities, like making the best possible choice. He was confident that he made the best and safest choice possible with the knowledge he had. But that didn't mean it left him free of responsibility.

He shook his head, dismissing such thoughts. Blaming himself during this situation will be a useless distraction. If he feels like it, blaming himself later is still an option.

If Karin was almost killed by a bear, what about other Genin roaming around? This forest was filled with dangerous and degenerate people. Shinji wasn't naive to the bad in this world. In this forest, the strong have power over the weak, whatever happens here stays here, if they kill the victim afterward.

"Can I help you with something else?" Muttered Karin, her cheeks red as she looked anywhere else but Shinji's eyes.

Bringing him out of his thoughts. He had seen the bite marks all over her body and somewhat was able to guess that there were a lot of painful things in this girl's life. With her healing ability and how it functioned.

'No wonder she wanted her teammates killed.'

"I still have Chakra, so if you need healing..." she glanced at him for a second, but looked away after meeting his eyes for a couple of seconds.

"No, I am okay," Shinji shook his head and instead looked North, where the tower is.

"Oh... okay," Karin looked down in disappointment.

"Stop thinking weird things," Sayuri interrupted her and then pointed towards Karin while addressing Shinji. "Also, what're we going to do with her?"

Shinji walked toward Karin, at first there was a trace of fear in her eyes. But then came acceptance, as a sweet, satisfied smile came to her face. "I am okay with this," she muttered to herself. "Getting killed by the guy I-"

Shinji picked her up like a sack of potatoes and put her over his shoulder. "C'mon we need to rush to the tower. We need to get out of here."

Normally he would have given her a piggyback ride, but he needed one of his hands free and it interrupted his reaction time toward the back. He couldn't see behind himself, but the cutting sound he kunai made in the air, the slight shift in the air, he needed to keep on guard. So this was the best way to carry her.

Sayuri stared at him as if she was looking at an alien. "Do you even understand human interactions? You're way too weird. All that training hasn't been good for your brain."

"What?" Shinji on the other hand looked at her weirdly too. But unlike Sayuri, he didn't bother looking into the situation too much. There is something more important to think about, like how to get out here and not confront people.

Kota, who had woken up, looked at his hand, clenching and unclenching his fist. He seemed in a trance, and Shinji knew that coming so close to death wasn't something easy to deal with.

"Kota, Sayuri, we have to go. Sayuri, you take care of the front," she had good senses and better hearing. Also if she carried Karin, then she would get tired since her stamina wasn't anywhere near Shinji's, as he could easily hold Karin and not inhibit his fighting abilities by getting tired. Plus, he had to keep an eye on Kota.

Fwish!

They started tree jumping, and Shinji's senses were sharp. He kept glancing at Kota every now and then.

'This was my fault. I made the wrong call going west and we were caught into an enemy trap.'

Maybe he should have gone and taken out Sasuke's team. They were undoubtedly the weakest, and he knew that he could handle them too.

Sayuri, as if reading his mind stated. "Don't worry about it. Your choice was the safest."

The thing was that he knew it too. There would be many other teams going after the weakest, and running straight to the tower would have been dangerous. Especially without having a scroll as you would have been just fish taking the bait. But now he could be stealthy.

"Ah, excuse me," Karin intervened. "I am a sensor and if you keep me safe I can sense quite far and have us not confront anyone until we reach the tower."

Shinji nodded, her value in his mind rose. Natural sensors like her were rare. "How far can you sense?"

"Normally around a hundred meters. But if I can concentrate and leave myself in your care, I can sense a little outside the Forest of Death."

Shinji almost stumbled at her answer. But hid his surprise. The whole Forest of Death? That was crazy long-range. He wondered if there was anyone else like her in Konoha? He somewhat knew about sensors, but even naturally gifted sensors can't sense Chakra even half that distance.

...

It took surprisingly little time to cross through the forest, and no team was encountered, mostly due to Karin's help. Shinji reasoned that maybe no one was desperate to make camp around the tower and wait for Genin to ambush, like a spider waiting for an insect to fly in its web.

But just as they got closer to the tower and were about to arrive into the vicinity.

"Three people to the right," Karin warned Shinji.

the sound of kunai cutting through the air rang in his ears, it was coming from the left. Shinji casually put down Karin and took out a kunai.

Clang! Clang! Clang! Clang!...

Each projectile was easily deflected, Kota had taken his sword out. Unlike his usual nonchalant self, the Genin now had a murderous gaze, peering towards where the kunai came from.

"Calm down," Shinji calmly instructed him. "The shots were too straight and had a sequence to them."

Due to not knowing who his enemies were, Shinji decided to keep Karin's sensory ability a secret.

From the opposite direction which the projectiles previously came from. A group of three Genin from Hidden Sand Village came out.

Shinji noticed that it wasn't the red-haired Genin and his team, as they seemed to be quite strong. But this group seemed somewhat normal, and amongst them was a puppet user who was using Chakra Strings to what essentially seemed like a doll little girls play with. Two of the guys had slicked-back hair and wore black, ripped cloth as face masks. The girl in the team had blue hair tied in a ponytail.

"Was that a mechanical object? That's cool, it made no noise either and I almost thought it was humans that were throwing the kunai." Shinji nodded with a gleam in his eyes. He tried to make himself seem as friendly as possible, since the enemies were now face-to-face, he didn't want to fight needlessly. He also already had the two scrolls his team needed. Fighting would only be a disadvantage to him.

How to turn this situation into something good? What Shinji wanted the most right now was information. But how to get that out of the opposing team? His mind worked a hundred thoughts a minute. He wasn't some smooth talker or charismatic leader. So the only way he can deal with this is by-

"How did you know?" The man was curious. The team had two men and a female amongst them.

'I wonder how long it would take me to kill them?' - wondered Shinji. '30 seconds? Maybe 10?'

Remembering the other Genin that he had killed, Shinji guessed that around twenty seconds, or maybe a minute at worst. This team likely passed the exam due to luck until now. Of course, he had no intention to kill them, but when meeting a potential enemy, it was better to think of how to kill them, only then he wouldn't be surprised.

Still, seeing that they were from the Hidden Sand village, and seeing a reason to eliminate another team, he approached them with a smile and offered. "I have an extra Heaven Scroll. I will give it to you for some extra information on certain examinees."

The teammates looked amongst themselves. Shinji wasn't worried about this extra team participating. They were weak, and he would rather have the information he needed. If they still wanted to fight, then he would oblige.

"What information do you need?" inquired the only female member in their team. "Also show us the scrolls as proof."

Shinji smiled and took out a Heaven Scroll, showing that he had it. On the other hand, he also showed that he already had a pair of scrolls.

'It seems like they require the Heaven Scroll. This is lucky for me, as I can finally get some genuine information that I need.'

"The red-haired guy from your village, who is he?" Shinji's question made the other team grimace. He could see the fear in their eyes and likely felt that he would kill them. At least that was what Shinji thought they felt. He wasn't going to try and change those notions, as fear can be useful in this situation to make them talk.

"Uhhh, there is not a lot known about him in general," muttered the girl, whose name was unknown until now. She glanced toward her teammates, and they nodded. "Though he is the son of the Kazekage, he also possesses the ability to control the sand in his gourd and the sand around him."

"They also say that he is the demon's spawn and has a demon inside of him," added one of the guys.

"That's just a rumor though." added the other guy.

At that, Shinji noticed Sayuri's eyes narrow, and her lips thin. "Go on," she prompted them. "Tell me more about this demon."

"O -Okay," the man to the left stuttered, he was the one who had mentioned the demon first. "Well, they say that the One-Tailed Tanuki Demon who lords over the desert sands. That's why they say he can control sand and his sand automatically coming to its protection is what people say is the demon protecting its host."

"Satisfied?" Asked the female teammate, her body was rigid and Shinji could tell she was still nervous. But he would hold his word.

This deal was beneficial for him, but the enemy was a sandbag he could hit in the next round if it involved any kind of fighting. Also, these weak enemies could end up revealing their opponent's abilities.

There was no real danger on his part, so Shinji decided to keep his part of the bargain. Glancing toward his team to see if they had any other questions for the Sand team, or opposed this decision. Seeing that they didn't, he threw his scroll right into the female teammate's hand, as he had deduced that she was likely the leader amongst them.

Shinji then turned toward Karin, with a gentle smile on his face. He planned to stay in the good graces of such a godly healer. If in the future he had an injury that might end his career, like some permanently cut tendons or muscles, he will go to her. "Let's go in the tower together, stick close, and as soon as we enter go to the top office and announce your resignation."

Karin's teammates were dead and there was no way she was going to pass the exam. But she would still at least spend some time in comfort in Konoha. Shinji was a little perplexed whether he should help her more, get her out of the terrible situation she is in. Did he have the ability to help her?

...

After that, he walked into one of the rooms and read a riddle about heaven and earth, Which showed how one should train their body or mind, depending on which aspect they were lacking. Shinji without even a second passing understood the riddle's meaning and threw the Heaven and Earth scrolls on the ground simultaneously.

Pooof

In a cloud of smoke, Kakashi came out, he was laying on the ground while reading a book. He looked up at Shinji and sighed. "Your team was the only one in Konoha that had to send a Jonin like me to handle you. Also yes, you would have been knocked out if you had opened the scrolls while in the forest."

Shinji felt like Kakashi was at a good part in his book. He had tried the Icha Icha Paradise books before, but they were mostly softcore smut. Very boring, as the plot mostly developed around the perverted protagonist.

"Really? But I think there were other people, like Lee's team that would need more than just a Chunin if they were to be knocked out without being harmed."

Kakashi's one eye stared at him and narrowed. "Stop trying to nit-pick."

"I'm just saying," Shinji shrugged. "I doubt we were the only team that had a Jonin summoning. Also why Yamato -sensei or Guy -sensei aren't here is because they trained me and might be biased in their actions."

Normally Shinji wouldn't take a risk and argue with a Jonin like this, as he didn't want to get on the bad side of a Jonin-ranked ninja. But from Guy, he had learned a lot about the Eternal Rival that he always spoke about.

"You're too troublesome," Kakashi sighed. "Anyway, you've passed the exam and have seven days of rest until the exam is over."

"Also, you've passed the Forest of Death in only eight hours, that's pretty good," he then smirked. "Still, you weren't first."

'Why does he seem amused by that? Did he make a bet or something? Was it Guy or Yamato -sensei? Guy doesn't seem like the kind of guy to gamble with something like money. Yamato -sensei probably would though.'

"Can you tell me who was first?" Shinji wanted to know who he should look out, for the most. Though he could somewhat guess a couple of people who were likely first, but didn't like making assumptions like that.

"That would be called favoritism. And I am anything but unfair."

Poof!

And just like that, the silver-haired Jonin disappeared in a puff of smoke, while laying down as he never took his eyes off the book while they talked.

Sayuri commented on Kakashi's behavior. "Glad we don't have him as our teacher, he looks lazy."

Shinji was a little iffy on that as while Kakashi might be a lazy teacher. He didn't know that as he had never been directly taught by Kakashi, but by the man's demeanor, there was a lot to say. But he remembered the one time the Jonin gave him some advice on hand-seals, it was very good and helped him tremendously.

sigh "Well, that was a rollercoaster of emotions," Sayuri added while side-glancing at Kota, who seemed out of it a little. In the Forest of Death, they didn't have time to try and reassure him.

Shinji, as the leader, bowed towards his teammates. "Sorry, Sayuri, Kota, it was my decision that led us to this situation. Especially Kota, you almost died because of my decision and I am willing to step down from my position as team leader."

To Shinji, being a team leader wasn't about just having the power to make decisions over his teammates. The title was nothing in his eyes. A leader is supposed to make the right decision, and he was willing to accept the responsibility that came with the good decisions, and he would do the same with the bad ones.

Since they were out of the Forest of Death, Shinji didn't want this to develop into a problem in the future so they had to talk about it now.

"Hahaha," suddenly Kota laughed. His weird, unreadable expression from before was gone. "I didn't know even you Shinji, could say something so stupid."

Then Kota's eyes turned sharp, veins crawling up his neck and forehead as if he was mad at something. "Don't blame yourself for my mistake. We were attacked, and as the weakest in the team, they attacked me. It's not your fault, and it's pissing me off just hearing you say that."

Shinji nodded. "Sorr-"

"Don't apologize!" His friend interrupted him. Looking down in disappointment at his hand. "The way I saw it, you didn't make the wrong decision. Instead, you saved my life and even healed me so no residue injured would cripple me. You stopped me from certain death. So stop apologizing, you made the best choice possible, and I agreed with it. Don't let such things ruin your mood, don't even think about it."

"For once, I agree with the knucklehead," Sayuri shrugged, pointing at Kota. "His life is his responsibility. Yes, as a team we help each other when we can, but during that initial attack none of us had the time to think about anything else other than to jump back and dodge."

After taking a breath, she added. "Also, in my opinion, your decision was the next. Going straight to the tower would have had us meet some dangerous people. The kind that could afford to charge straight to the tower. Going after Sasuke's team… Well, let's just say we wouldn't be the only ones."

She glanced around. Shinji, having known her quite well by now, it seemed like Sayuri wanted to say something but stopped herself and instead added. "They were the weakest team and other ninjas were bound to go after them. I thought your decision was the best too."

"Me too," Kota gave a thumbs up.

…

After walking out of the room they used the summoning scroll, a Chunin greeted them. Shinji remembered him as one of the gate guards. The man gave them a room number, which would be their resting place until the week was over and he also told them where they could order food and at which hours.

Walking to their room, it was a simple one-bedroom, three beds, and a bathroom door on the other side of the room. Except for beds and sheets, the room was relatively empty.

Kota was the first one to go and lay down into bed, moaning about how it feels like forever since he had slept in a bed, even though he had just slept yesterday in one. Due to finishing the exam so fast, Shinji and his team didn't need to camp out, or even hunt for food. Well, even if it came to that, they wouldn't need to go hunting since as a precaution Shinji had prepared 6 months of rations just in case… he likes being prepared for these kinds of situations. A whole storage scroll was filled with different-tasting ration bars.

'Better not needing it and having it, than needing it and not having it. Also, it isn't like the money spent on it was wasted as I can eat these nutritious ration bars after training.'

"Guys. I have to tell you something," Sayuri stated, interrupting both Shinji and Kota from their thoughts. "The Demon that the Hidden Sand team talked about. They exist. Also, let me warn you, they're very dangerous."

…

In their room, Sayuri explained what she knew about the tailed beasts and Jinchuuriki. Also dropping the bomb that Konoha's Junchuuriki was Naruto. Now Shinji had somewhat of an understanding of why the yellow-haired prankster had passed the Genin Exams even though he failed it at first.

'Now I have more dangerous knowledge about the village. I need to keep my mouth shut about this.'

While laying down in bed, many thoughts went through Shinji's mind. In the end, he contemplated what he would do for the rest of the week he had left.

He knew not to fatigue himself too much as there was an exam just around the corner, but a little training hurt nobody.

_____

[Choose one of the choices, and white it down in the comments below:]

A - Train Chakra Strings. An interesting technique, something that Sayuri introduced to Shinji. It could increase his Chakra Control to a level very few ninjas bothered to train at. Which might give him an edge during the next phase of the Chunin Exams.

B - Read some medical books. Today's situation with Kota has made Shinji anxious, seeing your friend bleed to death and knowing that he couldn't do anything. Today he was lucky to have Karin around. But what about next time something like this might happen?

C - Read Medical Books and Train Chakra Strings. Shinji is used to doing multiple things at the same time, and can even use it as training. (This option is available due to Multitasking Trait)

D - Talk with Yamato about Karin. You saw those bite marks and knew that her situation wasn't that good. Explain her ability, last name, and how she could be useful to the village and ask if it was possible to get her out of her situation and help her. A healer like that was nothing short of a miracle for him and his team. But Shinji deduced that Konoha has its dark side, like every hidden village, so he didn't want to bring her into a worse situation, but wants to get some advice about the situation from a Jonin he trusted. If it didn't work out, then he would do something else for the rest of the week. (If this vote wins. The second most voted choice will take effect if the talks fail or are too short.)

E - Spy on the other contestants and try to figure out their abilities.

_____

A/N: Join discord where I post the dice rolls of the chapter and their effects. And discuss with other readers about plans for Shinji:

https://discord.gg/wbwRTqd7jr

P.S: For every 150 Power Stones, Shinji gets a reroll in a bad dice roll. (which determines luck-related events). Also, the re-roll counter is on discord.

Chapter 25: Chapter 25 - Promise 3

[D] - Talk with Yamato about Karin.

***

Chapter 25 - Promise

...

As he lay down in his bed, Shinji's body was engulfed by the softness of the mattress and he relaxed a little. It was strange, he was usually used to his body aching from training when he went to bed, and never really got to appreciate just how nice it was to lay around sometimes.

Shinji went through many ideas and thoughts. Each new idea would get replaced by a plan, but they soon were dismissed. His mind couldn't help but think of a certain someone.

He never had thoughts of worrying about anybody in this life. But the red-haired girl, Karin, the one who had saved Kota's life. Shinji was grateful to her, Kota was one of his best friends, and a dear teammate.

Closing his eyes, Shinji could vividly remember the girl's arms, neck, and midsection. Full of bite marks, and the way she looked at her teammates, with anger and rage.

But what can he do? He isn't someone with a lot of influence or someone powerful.

"Whatcha thinking about?"

Turning around, he glimpsed at Sayuri, laying down on the bed, her long dark hair shuffling about as her soft blue eyes stared back at him.

She seemed relieved and happy. As if a huge weight had rolled off her shoulders.

"Don't tell me, you're going to train?" Sayuri asked, with a drained sigh. "It feels like we were in that forest forever. How about we rest for a change?"

"There's something worrying me. I don't know whether doing this is the best course of action." Shinji stated.

He didn't know a lot about the semi-politics involved with Ninja.

Maybe if he becomes a powerful ninja in the future he might have to get involved with that, but for now, such things are too far out of his reach.

So he planned to ask Yamato for some advice on what he should do next.

Shinji knew the reality of his situation, and how unimportant he was to anyone in the village and was just another disposable pawn.

People saw him as talented, but he knew the truth of that too, an illusion that will crumble as soon as he stops working hard.

Suddenly, the sound of air being cut by a thrown object tickled his ears. As a ninja, he was very sensitive like this, and before he could comprehend it, his body moved, recognizing that this wasn't the sound a kunai made when it was thrown.

Twisting his body, he caught the object by its tip, and by the time he registered what had happened. He noticed that it was a pillow. Shinji was still in fight or flight mode and contemplated throwing the pillow far away as it might have an explosive tag attached to it.

But he crushed such instincts with an iron fist as soon as they came.

He raised a questioning brow to Sayuri, the Pillow Thrower.

"You should relax. It's always about doing something with you."

A mischievous smirk danced on her lips, as she teased him.

He smiled back, glancing at the pillow on his hand. "You're stupidly smart somestimes."

"Hehehe, you're going to have to give up," she stood up, ignoring Shini's comment. With hands on her hips, she declared. "My ultimate pillow fighting technique is-"

Before she could finish, Shinji threw the pillow and with strength born from countless hours of training, the pillow flew through the air like a kunai and landed on her face. The momentum pushed her back down on the bed.

"Pah!" Her hair became disheveled, and she pouted. Her posture was like that of an annoyed cat ready to pounce.

"What? You can dish it out, but can't take it?" Shinji smirked, he also felt a warmness inside his chest. It was nice to have people care about you. In the orphanage, he was the average kid, the one that even the matrons rarely remembered his name.

Sayuri's eyes widened as she quickly glanced down. "Y, You should smile a little more."

Kota chuckled for some reason Shinji couldn't quite understand. The swordsman Genin glanced toward Shinji, and then back at Sayuri, his chuckle became even louder. "For all your intelligence you're quite oblivious sometimes."

Shinji tilted his head. "Oblivious? How? I am not the best out there, that's obvious. But between us, I was the one who always interacted with our clients in D Rank missions."

Kota suddenly got a mischievous smirk as he glanced at Sayuri. "Well, there's this girl and she has-"

He wasn't able to talk anymore, as Sayuri with agility she usually didn't use threw a pillow at such speed and power that Kota fell out of his bed. "I'll kill you if you say a word more."

Shinji was surprised by this. His team was fighting amongst each other?! He had never noticed this before, he always assumed that as a team they were quite friendly.

'I can think about this later, right now this needs to be stopped from escalating,' thought Shinji.

He was behind Sayuri within an instant, twisting her arm behind her back. "Calm down. We shouldn't be fighting amongst each other."

Sayuri squirmed under his grasp and tried to get away.

"L, Let go of me," she whined (?) Sayuri never whined. Also, her voice sounded soft and more girly than before.

"Bahahaha!" Kota for some reason found the situation hilarious. "Oh, God, this is too good! Bahahaha!" he was rolling on the ground while holding his stomach, barely able to breathe. "Shinji, you, you, Bahahahah! Sayuri, she likes you."

Sayuri's body immediately grew rigid within his grasp, and she didn't turn around to meet his eyes. With the firm grasp on her arm, Shinji felt Sayuri's pulse quicken.

'Was she worried about something?'

"Likes me?" Shinji was no fool and immediately caught on to what was going on.

Sayuri liked him? That's good because he liked her too, she has been an amazing teammate.

She always helped him in every turn of the way, and had always been there for him when he needed help.

"I like her too, she's an amazing teammate and friend," he declared with a smile.

"That's... okay..." Sayuri sighed and looked down in disappointment, while Kota chuckled like a mad man. How was he so full of energy? Two minutes ago he was almost ready to go to sleep.

Shinji shook his head at this. But he was happy, and the smile on his face wouldn't go away.

These small fleeting moments were something that made this team worth something in his eyes.

"Anyways, I'm going to try and find Yamato -sensei. I need to talk to him about something."

Sayuri's gaze became sharp at that, while Kota glanced at him too. But the latter was laying on his bed and ready to fall asleep, today hadn't been an easy day for him.

"I feel like you're going to do something I'm not going to like. Explain," her words were sharp like a razor.

Shinji saw no reason to hide this from her.

...

Shinji explained to his teammates about Karin and how he planned to try and convince Yamato -sensei to have her 'die' and join Konoha after her fake death. Or something like that.

Or at least that was the last resort as he didn't want to try and expose himself too much. She had saved Kota and Shinji was grateful to her and wanted to at least try and help her.

Sayuri stared at him and shook her head. "Shinji, this isn't a good idea to get involved with. You should know that you aren't that valuable to the village. Do you know what happened to the Hyuga Clan? They protected their clan members from being kidnapped and the Hokage still..."

She didn't need to say anything more as Shinji understood what she was getting at. This situation was dangerous. "Don't worry, I'm not going to sacrifice myself for Karin, or anything like that. It's just a simple request to Yamato -sensei."

"Promise me that if he refuses, you will accept that and move on," Sayuri insisted.

Seeing no response, she continued. "I know one day you will become a Ninja, like any rarely seen before. By then you can afford to save people. So promise me right now, that if Yamato -sensei tells you there's nothing he can do about it, then you'll drop this."

Shinji glanced toward Kota for his input. This could be a decision that will affect the whole team.

His friend stared at the ceiling deep in thought, before sighing and nodding. "I appreciate that she saved me. But I don't want something to happen to you because of me. So I agree with Sayuri."

*****

[Choose one of the choices, and white it down in the comments below:]

A - Accept Sayuri's promise.

B - Accept Sayuri's promise. (lie)

C - Don't promise Sayuri anything. This will anger Sayuri and Kota will be displeased.

***

A/N: Shinji is about as socially observant for certain things as a harem protagonist. His luck is really strange, almost always bad at small things like this.

Made in the USA
Columbia, SC
22 April 2024

34727074R00080